# THE
# CHIMPANZEE
# & ME

# THE CHIMPANZEE & ME

Ben Garrod

ZEPHYR

For all individuals in need of help, and for every individual who ever has helped. Regardless of species.

'All animals are equal but some animals are more equal than others.'

George Orwell, *Animal Farm*

# CONTENTS

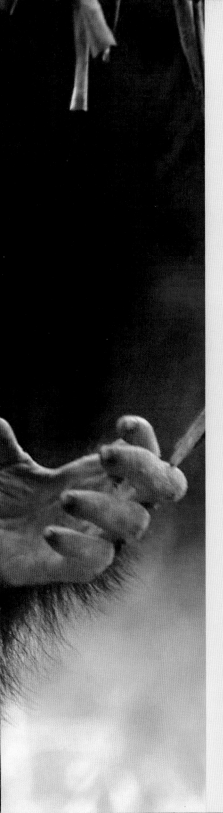

# PASA

---

## Where chimpanzees and me start our adventures

As Max explores the world around him, he reminds
me that the more time I spend with chimps, the less I
understand them. Who knows what he's thinking here.

I know it's a cliché to have a holiday romance but, in my defence, this was different. For a start, this wasn't a holiday, I was working. Secondly, and more importantly, she wasn't even the same species as me. In my head, this does make the whole thing that little bit better, if not admittedly a little bit weirder. Her name was Pasa and she was a chimpanzee.

I had landed the job of a lifetime, where I was off to run a large chimpanzee conservation project in the north-western part of Uganda, in East Africa. I was there to follow and habituate wild chimpanzees, develop staff training and community education programmes, aid law-enforcement efforts and implement an ambitious eco-tourism venture. It was my first job after graduating from university. I was ambitious (and an idiot) and can vividly remember thinking 'just how hard can it really be?' I would later find out *exactly* how hard it can be to follow wild apes who don't wish to be followed, live alongside a veritable who's who of deadly snakes and relive *that* scene from *Alien* every time a mango-fly larva hatched from my chest in the dead of night. Trust me, they're small in size but giants on the grossness scale. All this and much more was to come in the months and years ahead, but for now, I needed a crash course in basic Chimpology.[1]

I had been sent to an amazing sanctuary in the middle of Lake Victoria, about 15 kilometres from the coast of Entebbe. I had high hopes of learning the subtle nuances of chimpanzee behaviour, and assumed I'd gain not only an insight to the inner workings of our nearest living relatives but would also emerge with a fundamental understanding of human nature, altruism, sociality and culture. What actually happened was that I picked up poop. Literally. And there was an endless supply of it to shovel.

---

1 Chimpology is very similar to human psychology but the subjects are usually less inhibited, throw their own waste around and arguably still remain more cultured than many of their nearest living relatives. Think about it…

It soon dawned on me that becoming a chimp-whisperer would come later… long after I'd mastered the more fundamental understanding of husbandry needs. Thirty-nine rescued chimps lived on the island sanctuary, roughly 1 km² in size, which is apparently the combined size of 140 football pitches. Although this may sound like a lot of space per chimp, it's not. Considering that one adult chimpanzee needs approximately 1 km² of habitat to survive in the wild, it doesn't take a maths genius to see that even the best sanctuaries can never fully provide the space needed. The cost would be astronomical. Instead, they heavily supplement the chimps' lives. They are given food, because they would eat faster than the trees could regrow fruit, and they're encouraged to sleep in large caged sleeping quarters, complete with hammocks. I landed the thankless (and, as I said, endless) task of sweeping, shovelling and hosing down the sleeping quarters each morning, after the boisterous gang of chimps left for the forest, to reinvent the wheel, rewrite the entire works of Shakespeare or generally fight, play and annoy each other for the day.

The first few weeks of my work felt like all the classic stages of grief… *Shock*: 'I can't really be the *Poop Guy*, can I? I got a first at university and everything.' *Denial*: 'Hmmf, I'm sure no one handed Jane Goodall a shovel when she arrived in Tanzania.' And *Bargaining* wasn't too far behind: 'Hey mate, if you clean today, I'll repay you in beers. By the way, it looks as though Mawa has had a bad tummy. Sorry.' Finally, with a sense of Zen-like inevitability, I found *Acceptance*. I learned to appreciate my morning ritual and came to love the natural, aesthetic beauty of a good turd. And while I appreciate the benefits of roughage in my own diet, I was truly grateful for it being in the diet of the three dozen or so excitable captive chimpanzees. It was my quiet time of the day. The wonderful period after the cacophony of breakfast and before the mayhem of lunch. There were rarely any tourists around and the sanctuary staff were usually busy, taking care of any veterinary needs and ensuring the animals were safe and happy.

Like any young social primate that hasn't yet discovered an iPhone, chimpanzees love being outside. They'd whoop and leap and generally go 'full chimp' as they cannoned into their forest playground. Faced with that, why would you ever consider staying behind? Well, maybe if you were a little antisocial, or far too mature for all that aping around, or generally didn't think especially highly of your forest playmates. There was one young chimp who fitted this profile perfectly. Pasa. She had arrived at the sanctuary five years earlier, at a little over six months old, rescued from the northern border with the Democratic Republic of the Congo. As with so many sanctuary animals, not much is known about her time in captivity but it was evident that Pasa was no ordinary chimpanzee. She was different to the others. I watched her throughout my first few weeks and noticed a pattern. Where the others were loud and raucous, she was quiet and calm. Where they were impulsive and reactive, she was methodical and contemplative. Quickly breaking the golden rule drilled into every zoology student, I anthropomorphised her. I projected human qualities on to her and plastered her with insight, hopes, dreams and aspirations.[2] I used to make myself chuckle at the notion she had no idea she was a chimpanzee but instead was simply waiting patiently until we silly humans realised our mistake in locking up one of our own with those 'animals'.

It seemed that she was in the midst of a chimpanzee existential crisis. From an outsider's point of view, she was truly on her own in the

---

2 And I'd do it again in a heartbeat. As a scientist, I see the absolute necessity in objective thinking and not allowing feelings to influence experiments and research but, in real life, it has been impossible for me to spend time with very young animals from all over the world and not see examples of fear, greed, sadness and humour in the animal kingdom. I think to see animals purely as objects or, worse, merely as data points, means we as scientists will miss much of what is actually going on, and that means as people we will fail on a far bigger scale.

world. She did not really play with the other kids and would openly challenge adults.[3] She was the odd kid in the corner. She would often spend time alone in the holding area, while the others were away being chimps. Sometimes, she would sit in the paddock close to the electric fence that separated human and non-human primates and watch the world go by. Now, as you might imagine (and rightly so), there are endless rules and regulations in any great ape sanctuary, designed to keep everyone safe. One such example is that you *never* touch a chimp. Ever. The caregivers have contact with many of them, but only after years of building up experience and trust with these incredibly strong and potentially deadly animals. It wasn't a difficult rule, and yes, I did understand it: *never*, ever, ever touch the chimps. Under any circumstances. They might take your arm off. But I touched her. What was worse, no one was around to see me do it, or to apply the tourniquet when the inevitable happened.[4] She watched me as I swept up near the holding area and reached her hand through the thick, unyielding bars, her slender fingers outstretched, her palm turned to the sky. She looked at me and I at her. I can remember thinking there was no way I was going to fall for this, she could find someone else to maim. She surprised me by remaining there, silent and still. Any self-respecting chimp would have been frantically shaking their hand up and down in frustration, vocalising and smacking their lips together in increasing annoyance. Think three-year-old human approximately thirty seconds before a nuclear tantrum. Pasa, however, sat there, her eyes never

---

3 There are many ways to do this but for me, it was when she would confidently tug on the pendulous testicles of the big adult males as they walked past. Such behaviour is strictly for the boys, to sort out rank and status, not for scrawny girl chimps who haven't read 'An Idiot's Guide to Being a Chimp'. Believe me, there were often some very surprised-looking senior male chimps in the sanctuary.

4 What I did was wrong and stupid. I endangered myself and Pasa and in no way would I ever want you to risk something as silly.

leaving mine, that little outstretched hand unwavering. I have no idea how long I sat there, returning her stare (another faux pas by us both). I was looking into those shiny chestnut-brown eyes and a being was staring back. Yes, of course, an animal but we are all animals. I saw something so profound in those eyes – someone capable of so much, of things I had dismissed as unscientific ramblings, yet here it was before me. This really was a thinking, feeling, emotional being, more related to me than to any other animal on Earth.

With all the worldly experience I had gained during three years of undergraduate study and (more significantly) the two weeks of hands-on experience in the sanctuary, I used my professional insight as an animal behaviourist to predict how far she could reach through the bars.[5] As I gauged the point where our fingertips would barely touch, she reached out and grabbed me by the wrist, her delicate fingers holding me in a steely, vice-like grip. I have never had the 'my life flashed before me' experience but at that moment I discovered it could equally be applied to particular body parts, as I prepared to get used to the prospect of becoming a permanent 'lefty'. There are lots of myths and anecdotes about the legendary strength of chimpanzees. The standard accepted view was that they were over ten times stronger than us. We now know that they are *merely* between one and two times stronger, which is only minimally more comforting. Although the size of a four-year-old (human) child, Pasa was definitely as strong, if not stronger, than me. She pulled my hand closer to the bar and in a moment of calm clarity, I let her. I could only trust in her good will and benign intentions. That faith drained away as my fingers headed straight for her mouth. This whole experience lasted two or three seconds at most, but it seemed like forever. With hindsight, it's

---

5 It is worth remembering that any savvy chimp will never let you know exactly how far they can reach, so, for example, you will always leave that £20,000 camera just that 5cm too close.

incredible to realise how much you can remember about the age of tooth eruption and canine morphology in apes in such a short space of time. Imagine my surprise then when she kissed me.

Okay, it was hardly *Romeo and Juliet*, but she puckered her lips, placed them on the back of my hand and just kind of, well, kissed it. Then she released her grip. Of course, I should have snapped my hand away and never placed it in danger ever again, but I am a scientist and, as I said before, quite the idiot, so I left it there, which Pasa took as an invitation to groom. I have a couple of small pale scars and a good-sized freckle on the back of my right hand. She spent the next fifteen minutes intent on ridding me of the pesky freckle. Grooming is hugely important to many social primates and none more so than chimpanzees. It not only means that what we call ectoparasites, such as ticks and lice, are removed from the body but it is also an invaluable social behaviour, creating, reinforcing and strengthening social bonds between individuals. Admittedly, this is usually between individuals of the same species, but sometimes different species come together for a bit of parasite-picking, such as buffalo and oxpeckers and cleaner wrasse and reef sharks. And now, to add to that list, a tiny chimpanzee and a clueless zoology graduate. This was not symbiosis at its best. One of the most wonderful things about science is that singular sense of discovery. Even if a thousand others have thought it, felt it or seen it before you, the feeling that you *might* be the first on to something new is always inspiring. It's what got me into science as a kid and is what keeps me 'sciencing' now. It makes me smile to recall wondering for the first time how all the wood pigeons 'knew' the same song when they were in different parts of the country, and I thought I'd discovered the key to unlocking the secrets of animal behaviour and that, before long, I'd be able to communicate with everything from gulls to goldfish. Okay, don't laugh, I was only about seven years old. And I roll my eyes remembering the time I watched a mother deer eat her own placenta,[6] thinking that I'd discovered cannibalistic (and possibly somehow even zombie) deer and should probably alert the authorities before they came for us. Okay, now you can laugh, I was about twenty-two years old. My experience with Pasa was the same. Here I was with a chimpanzee, socialising and positively communicating between species. I'd read work by the greats such as Dian Fossey and George Schaller on gorillas, Birutė Galdikas on orangutans and, of course, as many books and articles as I could find by Jane Goodall, and my literary, primate-loving heroes all mentioned 'breakthrough moments' with apes. This was my own bio-anthropological moment of clarity. Never mind that I didn't especially come to any real conclusions, or that, as I'd later realise, Pasa was quite free with her grooming affections to any human who gave her even half the chance. It's worth saying that if you do ever find yourself in the surreal situation of being groomed by a chimpanzee, it is of paramount importance to remember that, like so many things in life, it's all about give and take. Any self-respecting chimp isn't about to clean those imaginary ticks off you if you're not prepared to clear imaginary ticks off them too. Also, you'll need some pretty convincing acting skills, because you have to regularly 'find' a tick and excitedly pick it off their skin, noisily smack your lips and pretend to eat it, obviously. It never gets old doing this.

I'd read the books, watched the documentaries and seen chimpanzees in zoos for years but this brief encounter with Pasa changed me profoundly. I have a slight confession, something I've never actually told

---

6 For a time, I was a field assistant on a very well-established research programme and spent my days endlessly watching wild deer give birth. My job was to note where mothers left their newborns and then help tag the calf. This blew my mind and did two things for me: first, it made me question whether any of us can truly be veggies and two, showed me that there are a lot of jobs out there that your school careers advisor probably won't tell you about.

anyone, but I'm trusting you. I didn't want to go to the sanctuary. In fact, I was dreading it and only saw it as a means to an end. I was a snob, a real 'bio-snob', in that I only wanted to work with wild animals, not those locked up. I felt bad, but for me it was simple; they just weren't the same as their wild counterparts, and in my naive and idealistic brain, they somehow didn't seem as *real*. But here, on this tiny emerald speck in the middle of a huge watery expanse, I very definitely had my mind changed. As it changed from Pasa trying to scratch the melanin from my body to me sorting through her hair in search of imaginary ticks and other delights, it seemed that I had finally started to understand something about nature. Something I might never have realised had Pasa and I not met, or had she decided to be more sociable (with her own species) that day, or had I even an ounce of sense and not touched her. Regardless, I really believe this encounter changed me. It cemented my love for the natural world and consolidated what I assume will be a lifetime's affinity with chimps. It also woke me up to the plight of conservation and the role that sanctuaries can (and do) play in ensuring the survival of the iconic animals that we love. For some, that might be pandas or moon bears, pangolins or sloths but for me, chimpanzee sanctuaries are special.

Roughly a hundred years ago, chimpanzees were found in twenty-five sub-Saharan African countries and although we'll never know for sure, the population was thought to be as high as two million individuals. Now, they have been eradicated from four of those countries and, in total, we would be lucky if even as many as 300,000 are left (many estimates put the number at around half this). Chimpanzees are in trouble. It's easy to talk about population decline and trends, or to say they are being lost, but this desensitises what is really happening and we should be *more* sensitised about it and then incensed by it. Chimps are being extirpated, not lost. They're being systematically killed for a whole host of reasons and where they are not being intentionally hunted for bushmeat or taken as pets, then they are simply collateral damage in the global malignancy that is habitat destruction, losing food and territory as their forest homes are cut and burned for timber, charcoal production, mineral mining, the unsustainable palm oil industry and an almost endless list of other demands. There is no question that there are plenty of species (even just within the mammals) worse off than chimpanzees. The International Union for Conservation of Nature (IUCN), which coordinates conservation efforts for species around the world and produces the Red List detailing the threat status against each listed species, states that of the 41,000 or so plant and animal species on the list, around a third are threatened with extinction. For primates, that number shoots up and approximately 60 per cent are facing the threat of extinction. With only around twenty-six individuals left in the wild and none in captivity, China's Hainan gibbon is a dire concern. The vaquita, the world's rarest porpoise, now numbers below thirty, as scientists and conservationists battle, seemingly in vain, to save this iconic little Mexican cetacean. There are too many mammals, birds, reptiles, fish, invertebrates, plants, corals, fungi hanging over the abyss of extinction, but for me, yet again, chimpanzees are different. What hope do we have of saving a desert ecosystem or a rare butterfly if we can't protect an archetypal species of great ape? Why should we care about the fate of swifts or invest in safeguarding fish stocks if we can't galvanise ourselves to save our closest living relatives? The chimpanzee is a benchmark. If we allow an animal that is genetically closer to us than it is to a gorilla to slip into the history books, then we have little hope of saving the countless other equally deserving species, habitats and ecosystems. Within science, we constantly debate whether they feel emotions like fear, sorrow or shame, but there is no question that we feel these things and I feel filled with all three at the thought that our insatiable species might just sit and watch as our forest cousins disappear forever.

That day, Pasa took away the idea that scars and freckles are stubborn opponents, and I learned the value of sanctuaries and the power of an individual. Whether human or non-human, the impact of the lone voice can be immeasurable. It can stir us deeply, force us to think, to act and to change. She also helped me see that despite thinking I was a researcher through and through, I was, in my heart, a conservationist and I promised her that I would do what I could to help. Then I met the Desmonds. I had been 'up country' for several months, learning about life with wild chimps, such as how there are a hundred and one ways to cook goat and rice[7] and why walking alone at night in the forest with your torch off to 'find yourself' isn't the best idea when that forest is practically filled to the rafters with leopards. I'd discovered that the true definition of cabin fever is not talking to the geckos at night but when you laugh at their replies. It's fair to say that I needed to leave the forest for a bit. Our charity headquarters were in Entebbe and after six hours in a matatu,[8] I was ready for some fine cuisine (or at least, a pizza and a beer). One of the lovely things about our HQ (or 'Chimp House', as it is fondly called) was that at any time, any number of random and fascinating human guests might be there. I had met famous chimpanzee researchers, compassionate bankers (one of the rarer species) and esoteric artists. Life was never dull at Chimp House. On this occasion, a new couple nestled among the usual suspects at dinner. Jimmy and Jenny Desmond. I fell in love with them before we'd even started eating. Both from the United States, Jenny is slight and radiates confidence and warmth. She's passionately intense, quick to laugh and one of the most dedicated people I have ever met. Jimmy, in contrast, is about the height and build of a small giraffe, with unruly hair covering his head and most

---

7 Despite it always tasting the same.

8 This is like a minibus but differs fundamentally in that it seems almost obligatory for a matatu to feel like a sauna on wheels, find every single pothole in the road (otherwise where's the fun in having no suspension), and always be filled to at least twice its actual physical (or legal) capacity with people, chickens and, of course, goats.

An extended family. The Desmonds have moved across the globe to care for orphaned chimpanzees in Liberia.

of his face, and a raucous laugh, and although he may come across as a 'dude', he's razor-sharp and respected internationally for what he does. Within minutes, I loved being around these guys. This meeting seems ages ago now but I still think exactly the same about them both, although they are now a combination of dear friends and extra siblings that I never knew I wanted and wouldn't change for the world. Jimmy was a veterinarian, gaining experience in working with great apes. Jenny was a brilliant photographer and had worked in marketing but wanted to work with sanctuary animals. Well, they were in the right place. They're a killer combo and with Jenny's additional skill as a photographer, it seemed inevitable that the Desmonds would one day find themselves in the situation they are now in, looking after the rarest chimps on the planet while coordinating the development of a world-class sanctuary, and tackling the illegal killing and trading of these great apes. Over the remainder of my time in Uganda, we crossed paths often. We never worked together and I'm not even sure they made it to my forest project while I was still there, but we had fun nevertheless. Meeting up invariably ended in shenanigans and even now, one of my nearest near-death experiences was white-water rafting down the Nile with the Desmonds. As it is so prone to doing, time moved on and life changed. I left Africa in 2007 and moved to Asia for a year to try to help save those big hairy orange cousins of chimpanzees in Sumatra. After orangutans, I ended up working in the Arctic[9] and then went looking for extinct rats in the Caribbean.[10] I did my PhD and sold my soul by trading apes for monkeys for a while and got to a point where I felt further from both chimpanzees and Africa than ever before. Then, in 2015, I heard from the Desmonds again. We had kept in touch over the years, but it was in no way enough. As I'd gone after orangutans and walruses, their lives had been equally eclectic (and hectic). After living and working practically everywhere, from Kenya and Uganda to Bangladesh and China, they arrived, along with their trusty sidekick Princess the dog, in western Africa. After a brief visit, they not only fell in love with Liberia but saw the potential, and need, to help chimpanzees there. As so often happens within conservation, they went for one reason but ended up staying for another, completely different, reason. Jimmy and Jenny found themselves caring for a number of ex-research chimps, who lived on a series of islands on the coast. They made a huge difference to the lives

---

9 Another one of those 'long stories' for another time, but I'd like to think I'm one of the very few primatologists to have ended up working in the High Arctic. It was definitely less humid.

10 Before you ask, no, I didn't find any – 'extinct' is a definitive term.

of these animals and are undeniably responsible for their survival and for their happiness. But Liberia and that tricksy forest god, *Pan,* had other ideas. There is always the goal of forging good working relationships with the local authorities and finding the government supportive. It is still something of a surprise when this dream comes true, but it's exactly what happened in Liberia. Word got out about this dedicated pair of chimp-chasers and the Forest Development Authority, which is the government institution responsible for sustainably managing (and conserving) all forest resources for the benefit of present and future generations in Liberia, got in touch. There were baby chimps being sold as pets at busy junctions in Monrovia, being found in markets and confiscated at roadside checkpoints across the country. There simply wasn't anywhere (or anyone) in the country who could care for them. Until now. Even people who owned chimps were handing them over to Jenny, sometimes driving to the house to do so. Without planning to, the Desmonds found themselves with what seemed suspiciously like the start of a chimpanzee sanctuary. With a supportive (human) community and the urgency of the plight of the rarest subspecies of chimpanzees, for which Liberia is a stronghold, they had an opportunity too good to miss. The project moved full steam ahead: they would develop, build and fill Africa's newest chimpanzee sanctuary. Plans were made, proposals drawn up and applications for grants filled out.[11] The decision was made to live in Liberia, both realising that their undertaking to help save the western chimpanzee was a lifelong commitment. Before long, an official charity was set up and Liberia Chimpanzee Rescue & Protection (LCRP) was born. Now there is a place of safety for orphaned chimpanzees and, through

---

11 It costs hundreds of thousands (if not millions) of pounds to develop a sanctuary like this, and every year it takes around £5,000 to keep each orphan happy and alive.

Sitting with Jenny, Star is intrigued by the other little chimp in the phone camera. Like us, chimps are into selfies in a big way.

successful confiscations, the Forest Development Authority and police are able to secure criminal convictions for those caught smuggling, trading and killing great apes in Liberia.

The trickle of new orphans turned into a flood. Every week or two, yet another emotionally and physically damaged young chimp arrived. To many, it may sound like a dream – baby chimps everywhere, filling your home with hairy, noisy energy. It's not. Because behind every cute face, adorable giggle or endearing food grunt is a little being who has been torn from its family, mistreated and often hurt. Arriving at a place like LCRP is just the start of months or even years of recovery. There are so many different characters there already, and a few minutes with Jenny and Jimmy is enough to see that they love them all. Each has a unique blend of naughtiness, energy and intelligence. Max is small for his age but fails to see this as a problem. He is confident and clever, usually the first into trouble, but has a gentle side a mile wide. He flips easily between frantic buzzing energy and wanting nothing more than a good cuddle and some quiet time. I'd be surprised if Max doesn't become the group alpha one day. It seems this confident mini-alpha's only weakness is fear of abandonment. He hates being left – which means he was probably alone a lot until he was saved by Jenny.

Bui is older than Max and the pair were inseparable for a while. Bui is a sweet kid and seems to be the favourite of many of the humans[12] involved with LCRP. He's the sort of kid that, if he were human, would be referred to as 'well-rounded'. Of course he's naughty, he's a chimp. But he's also tender and gentle. He's never going to be top of the class at anything needing record-breaking intelligence but he finds his own way of doing things. I like Bui, because there's always a lot going on behind his pale brown eyes.

Poppy is also known as Picky (or even Picky P) because she's fussy as to who she'll tolerate near her, whether human or chimp. The truth is that Poppy has trust issues and I dearly hope she'll get over them. I love watching her. She'll stare at the others or watch an activity with unremitting intensity, taking everything in, assessing (and probably judging) it all. Poppy really is fearless. I've seen her wade into the middle of play-fights, where everyone then walks off scolded and abashed, and have myself been on the receiving end of her ire. When we first met, I received several 'Poppy nips',[13] as she was less than happy about me playing with the others. We get along fine now, but back then I apparently wasn't trustworthy.

If Poppy is fearless, then baby Ella is an old soul in a young body. Unlike her older playmate, who angrily breaks up fights and games, Ella leaps in just because she can. She wants to be involved with everything and doesn't realise that such young chimps shouldn't climb nets or swing on ropes quite as readily as she does and seems to operate on the principle, 'Well, if you're doing it, then why can't I?' Chimpanzees

---

12 As opposed to those non-human people who are also part of the project.

13 The sort that involve teeth.

often make distinct calls when they eat. They're called food grunts and sound like a really emphatic 'Mmmmmmm', which trails off. I can wholeheartedly say that this tiny bundle makes the loudest and most energetic food grunts I've ever heard. She only has to see a piece of fruit and she's off. It makes me chuckle every time.

Jojo. Oh, Jojo. It's hard to know where to start with this young chap. I'm always wary of promoting stereotypes and perpetuating the idea that chimps make good pets, so I don't like to describe them as 'clowns' or 'goofy', but Jojo is. I've never met a funnier animal. Even his face cracks me up. It seems a little longer than it should be, and he often sits with his mouth open and lower lip curled down. There was some question as to whether he was okay when he arrived, but it soon became apparent that young Jojo is just different to most chimps, swinging to a different drumbeat. I have watched him on his own, slowly ambling across the grass, suddenly stopping, spinning round and round, twisting wildly, arms flailing. On and on he'll dance, until he finally falls down, dizzy and happy, before carrying on across the grass as if nothing had happened. The others seem to love him and if anybody wants a game, they know where to go.

There are so many others, who are equally wonderful in their own way. Survivor is a big happy lad. He plays rough and it's clear he spent a fair amount of time in the forest but is settling in to life in the sanctuary. Gola, Rebecca and Lei Lei are roughly the same age and, along with Gloria, make up a team of confident girls, inseparable and tough. Lucy is slightly older and one of the most intelligent young chimps I've met. Connie came in with malaria and shrapnel injuries from when his mum was shot but has recovered well and spends his days hanging out with his best pal, Lucy. Portia, who, it's hard to deny, is a bit of troublemaker, and Chance, who scared everyone when she came in with injuries so bad that no one knew whether she'd survive, all help make up this wonderful great ape equivalent of the Lost Boys

Never a dull moment. As the only vet for miles, Jimmy cares for chimps, puppies, monkeys, vultures and anything else in need of help.

(and girls). They and plenty of others are part of a large group and have years ahead of them to play, fight, groom, eat and thrive with one another.

The project is, in some ways, already a victim of its own success. With more and more chimps arriving, Jenny and Jimmy knew that, as they matured, the orphans would need a proper space to live and that this should be as similar to wild habitat as possible. Luck has been on their side, because a patch of land within a coastal delta became available. Set among vast mangroves, this new site is perfect. Cut off on three sides by a wide, slow river, they only need to secure the fourth side to stop the chimps escaping into unsuitable areas and becoming lost or hurt. The forest is thick and wild, with trees to climb, vines to swing on and enough foliage to make a nest each night. There's wild food and paths through the undergrowth. Perfect chimpanzee habitat. The plan is to build a sanctuary with a veterinary clinic, staff quarters, educational facilities, opportunities for eco-tourism and a big sleeping area for the chimps to come back to each night. It's a new life for everyone involved and will make LCRP in line with the very best ape sanctuaries found in Africa. I said 'will' because they're not quite there yet. As well as wrangling nearly forty chimps in a less than ideal situation right now, the Desmonds are working around the clock to make this move happen. Jenny never stops applying for grants and securing donations and Jimmy is the only wildlife vet within the country, coordinating everything from work on rabies to Ebola research. My big hope is that not long after my book hits the shelves, Jenny, Jimmy, the team of amazing care-givers and other staff, and of course all the chimps will move to their new forest home.

And me, what's my role? I've written this book trying to look at everything that currently affects wild chimpanzees around the world but I've centred it wherever possible around the work the Desmonds are doing. So much of what they're achieving can be rolled out to

Expert care. Gola and the other orphans benefit from the care of Princess and the other ex street dogs at the sanctuary.

highlight what's going on with our nearest living relatives and what the future might hold for them. Over the course of a year or so, I have regularly visited Liberia to see the Desmonds and have watched the chimps as they grow, settling into their first year or two at LCRP. During my time there, I've laughed (a lot), cried, and have been filled with hope, despair and passion. I've had the opportunity to fall in love with chimpanzees all over again, have caught up with some very dear friends and have made some lifelong new ones (from various species) along the way. I've been given an extraordinary opportunity to spend time with this wonderful species and decided that the best way to help them is to share their story here. I hope you enjoy it.

Happiest outdoors. The author trekking gorillas in Uganda. The smile may have faded a little after still trekking eight hours later.

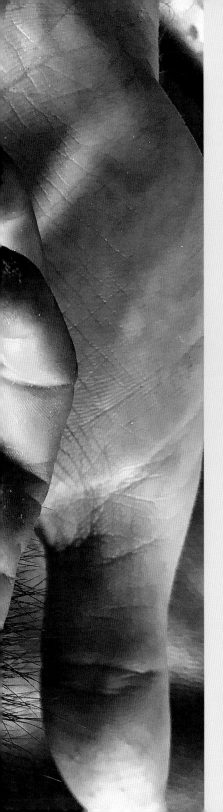

# I'M 98.6% CHIMP

---

## So what actually is a chimpanzee?

Same but different. The hands and feet of a chimpanzee are so similar to our own, even down to the unique prints.

It takes a lot to annoy me (unless you're my little brother) but the question guaranteed to make me go ape is, 'Well, if we *did* evolve from chimpanzees, how come there are still chimps, hey?' It made me sigh even typing that. It annoys me because a lot of people use it as a silly (and wrong) argument to try to rubbish the idea of evolution first of all ('pfft, as if we evolved') and that humans might actually be animals. Let me say it here; yes, we evolved and yes, we are animals. More than that, we are part of the ape family. We are like chimps but no, we did not evolve from them. Instead, we both evolved from something[1] we call a common ancestor between five and seven million years ago. The best way to think about it is like this – within your own family, a common ancestor for you and your brother (or sister) might be your granny. You both descended from her but you never used to actually be her, and as soon as you were both born, she didn't suddenly cease to exist, did she? Basically, humans have never been chimpanzees and chimpanzees have never been humans. Okay, it's a little more complicated, but if you understand that, then you're getting there. Oh, and as for the 'well, if humans are so great, then why are there still chimps, why didn't they just evolve?' – they *have* been evolving all the time that we have and, like us, they are perfectly adapted[2] for the habitats and environments in which they live.

Before we look at what a chimpanzee actually is rather than what it isn't (as in, it definitely is not your direct ancestor), it might help to do a great ape mugshot. Imagine all great apes alive today are in some sort of weird police line-up.[3] The big gingery orangutan from Asia is on the

---

1 We still don't know what this ancestor might have looked like yet… to be fair, it would have probably looked more chimp-like rather like your great great great (add a few more 'greats' here) granny or grandad but with more hair.

2 Well, we're far from perfect, actually. In fact, humans are a bit rubbish in lots of ways. If I had my way and was in charge of evolution, I'd redesign our bad backs, our dodgy knees and a whole host of anatomical errors left over from a four-legged past.

3 I have no idea what sort of crime would have me confused with an orangutan or a gorilla (a chimp, maybe) but hear me out on this train of thought.

far right, his small eyes and dark leathery face framed by a shock of fiery red, giving him the ultimate 'just out of bed' look. Next up, the gorilla. His broad flat nose and jutting mouth make him look as though he'd be the last thing you'd want to meet on a dark forest pathway, but this gentle silvery-haired giant is far from aggressive. Next come the more diminutive features of the chimpanzee, much shorter and smaller in stature than the other unusual suspects in this bizarre and unique line-up. The speckled face is framed by oversized comedic ears and a wide toothy grin, giving the chimpanzee an instantly recognisable look. Finally comes the human. Tall and spindly, mostly hairless and generally strange-looking. The muscles are nothing special and are definitely not well adapted for a life in the trees and the flattened face makes this strange species stand out from the other apes. Although each of these hominids[4] share similarities, it is plain that the human is the odd one out. It may come as a surprise, then, that at a genetic level, the chimpanzee is more related to the human than it is to the gorilla. Let that sink in for a second. Orangutans split off from the main trunk of the family tree some 15.7 million years ago, leaving the rest of us to show what a close family looks like. Gorillas went their separate way and split from a common ancestor around 8.8 million years ago, leaving the mystery human–chimp ancestor to go it alone for a while,[5] until what would become the human and chimpanzee lines split from one another, and our mysterious human–chimp last ancestor dawdled its way into the prehistory books.

---

4 A hominid refers to a level of biological classification (or taxonomy) which covers the orangutans, gorillas, chimpanzees, humans and all of our immediate (and sadly extinct) human ancestors, such as the enigmatic Neanderthals.

5 It's worth remembering here that the orangutan didn't suddenly split off, leaving the gorillas to decide to go their own separate way. At each junction (or branch), an often-unknown common ancestor split each time, with one branch evolving into gorillas, for example, and the other branches leading to all subsequent members of the family.

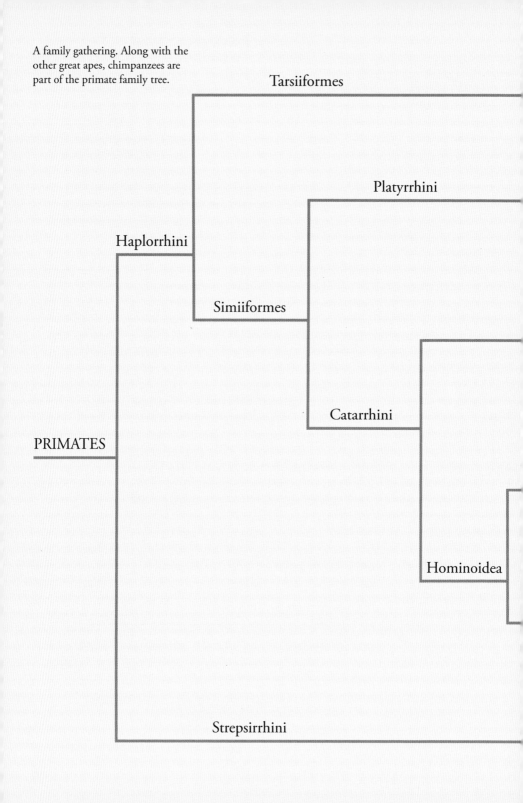

A family gathering. Along with the other great apes, chimpanzees are part of the primate family tree.

Tarsiiformes

Platyrrhini

Haplorrhini

Simiiformes

Catarrhini

PRIMATES

Hominoidea

Strepsirrhini

Tarsiers

'New World monkeys' such as spider monkeys, capuchins and tamarins

Cercopithecoidea 'Old World monkeys' such as mandrills, baboons, macaques and guerons

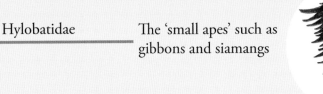

Hylobatidae The 'small apes' such as gibbons and siamangs

Hominidae The 'great apes' such as orangutans, gorillas, bonobos, chimpanzees and humans

Lemurs, Loris, bushbabies

This great (ape) family tree reveals not only our closest living relatives but also our sometimes surprising relationships between the branches, highlighting the pitfalls of judging a book by its cover and the concept that while you might not be a monkey's uncle (or aunt), you are a chimpanzee's cousin. Although the exact figure is argued and tossed about laboratories and classrooms around the world, it is thought that humans and chimpanzees share 98.6 per cent of their genetic blueprints, making them closer in at least a molecular sense than many subspecies.[6] Some scientists have even called for a reclassification and for either *Homo troglodytes* or *Pan sapiens* to be introduced to the world. If you haven't yet figured it out, it is currently *Homo sapiens* (that's me and you) and *Pan troglodytes* (that's chimpanzees). Considering there are currently several subspecies of chimpanzees – *Pan troglodytes troglodytes* (the 'central' chimpanzee), *Pan troglodytes verus* (the 'western' chimpanzee), *Pan troglodytes ellioti* (the Nigeria-Cameroon chimpanzee) and *Pan troglodytes schweinfurthii* (the 'eastern' chimpanzee) – and that the *Pan* branch leading to chimpanzees split and evolved before the relatively recent new kid on the block '*Homo*' branch, should we humans go for a major PR rebranding and become a fifth chimpanzee subspecies: *Pan troglodytes sapiens*?

While I am not suggesting we rethink our legal and evolutionary viewpoint to such an extent, it does give us much food for thought: does something so closely related to us deserve if not human rights, then 'nearly human' rights? How would this impact the use of chimpanzees in the entertainment industry and the world of biomedical research? Would those companies that cut down the forest homes of wild chimpanzees face the same legal consequences as someone who randomly knocked your home down one day? This may seem a bit

---

6 If two groups of organisms are more closely related than two separate species, they can be considered as subspecies. Although definitions here are famously vague, one loose guideline is that whereas species usually can't breed and make offspring which can then go on to breed, subspecies often can.

bizarre to discuss here but the truth is that some countries are already giving special rights to chimps because they *are* so different from almost every other non-human animal[7] on the planet.

It may not come as a huge surprise that I am a bit of a geek. Just one of the many ways in which my geekiness manifests itself is that I love to collect old, leather-bound zoology textbooks. I search for old books everywhere I go and end up spending a lot of time reading them and making sure the clothes moths in my home don't expand their diet. I have a lot of old books on my bookshelves. In among them is *Man's Place in Nature*. It was written in 1863 (although mine was printed in 1929) by Thomas Henry Huxley. It's a little black book, leather-bound and perfectly sized to fit in your pocket. It looks a little bit boring but within it is all we knew about chimpanzees, the other apes and human evolution around 150 years ago. And wow, did we still have a long way to go back then. This little book came out just four years after the most famous naturalist ever, Charles Darwin, published *The Origin of Species*, where he recorded how he (rightly) believed that each generation of organism across the natural world (from butterflies and sharks to oak trees, spiders and human beings) passes on teeny-tiny mutations to the next generation that have either a physical or behavioural way of showing themselves, such as a slightly longer neck or the ability to solve problems more quickly, *if* these mutations help increase their chances of survival. In other words, if they are an advantage in any way, they are passed down and, over time, some become more and more exaggerated, like the giraffe and its long neck (because this didn't happen after one hungry ancient giraffe ancestor kept stretching her neck) or sardines swimming in shoals so dense they can be seen from space.

The earliest reference I can find to a chimpanzee is from 1598 by an Italian explorer called Filippo Pigaletta. He had heard the story of their

---

7 Because remember, we *are* animals too.

existence from a Portuguese sailor and the way the explorer describes chimps was pretty rubbish. However, there is a drawing, of an old man chasing what looks like two young chimps around a tree. Obviously, people from Africa knew about chimps for thousands of years before this but it was (I think) the first time one had been described both in (slightly) scientific detail and also within a book. This may or may not have been the first time chimpanzees were described but what is self-evident is that afterwards we didn't really know what a chimpanzee was for a while. Sometime later, Edward Tyson, who was both a doctor and a scientist, had a good go at describing chimpanzees properly. In 1699, he wrote that the '*hair was of a coal-black colour*' and '*when it went as a quadruped on all fours, 'twas awkwardly; not placing the palm of the hand flat on the ground, but it walk'd upon its knuckles*'. Part of the problem was that lots of different people were trying to describe all these new ape species but, also, a lot of the people were basing their descriptions on what other people had seen. If you don't know what I mean here, then imagine describing a giraffe to someone who's never seen one: 'Yeah, it's like a horse but with blotchy spots and horns and oh yeah, a neck longer than a car'… See, it can be hard to think about an animal that has never been described before. We had a few problems with gorillas[8] but chimpanzees seem to have had a million different names. Looking in old books, there they're called Morrous, Boggoes and even Pygmies. The most common name for these little black African apes was Engeco and this name stuck for a while before 'chimpanzee' was used in the first half of the eighteenth century. Even then, many people, including a fair few scientists, thought orangutans, gorillas and

---

8 Before it was known as the gorilla, it was known as a Pongo. Sounds a cool name but it's the genus name we now use for orangutan, such as *Pongo abelii*. We also thought gorillas were aggressive and killed people and ate them… it sounds much better to survive an encounter with *that* sort of animal rather than with a gentle vegetarian that farts a lot.

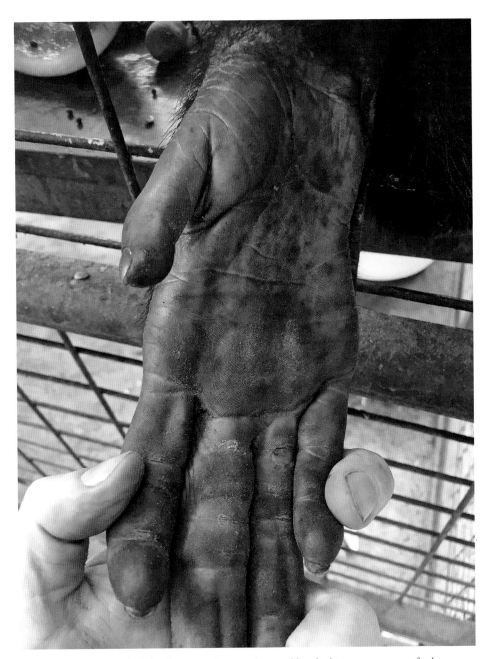

A helping hand. Through slight changes such as an elongated hand, chimpanzees are perfectly adapted to life in the forest.

chimpanzees were all the same animal.[9] It took about 250 years to sort out that gibbons and all of the great apes were different from one another, and even during the eighteenth century, chimps were commonly known as Jockos. It was only when scientists who specialise in anatomy, such as Edward Tyson, that we really started to understand chimpanzees. Finally, after more than two centuries, we were beginning to realise what a chimpanzee actually was.

So, it is becoming clear that it's not actually very clear what separates us from chimpanzees. It took about 250 years to decide that they were different from orangutans, remember. They're more like us than any other animal, but as scientists, we need to answer the question, 'What *exactly* is a chimpanzee?' What separates them from monkeys, for example, and how are they different from gorillas? Most importantly, what are the things we can investigate to help us look in a mirror and be certain it's not some odd hairless chimpanzee staring back? To answer these questions, we need a quick biology lesson.

First of all, chimpanzees are not monkeys, they are apes.[10] They're very closely related to monkeys, however, and along with the prosimians,[11] they make up the primates. Primates can be separated from all the other mammals by a bunch of different adaptations (or changes in their anatomy or behaviour). These primate adaptations

---

9 This may sound silly but, in fairness, we also thought that there was another species of human called the 'cat-tailed people'. No prizes for guessing which extra body part they apparently had. They also apparently ate people. The rule here is don't always believe what you're told by people who have been on crazy adventures and have apparently found bizarre new species of animals. Always ask for proof.

10 While some people argue that, by some scientific definitions, they are in fact monkeys, for the purposes of what we're talking about now, they're not. Taxonomy is strange like that and under the same criteria, birds are technically reptiles. Don't ask.

11 Literally meaning 'before monkeys', the prosimians includes the lemurs, bushbabies (or galagos), pottos, lorises and tarsiers.

Staring into the mirror. Looking into the warm and intelligent eyes of Ace is a humbling and somewhat life-changing experience.

used to identify the group aren't rules, they're guidelines, because there are nearly always exceptions. It is important to remember that with primates, almost more than any other group of mammals such as the bears, whales or cats, it's nearly all about the hands and feet… and maybe the eyes too. Remember, these things are true for *most* primates, so don't start thinking of ones that don't fit just to prove me wrong.

**33**

They have grasping hands and feet with opposable big toes and thumbs, with five digits on each hand and foot. An exception are the spider monkeys from South America, which only have four fingers on each hand, making them perfect hooks for swinging quickly through trees.[12] Instead of hooves or claws, like many other mammals, primates have nails. Some species, though, such as the beautifully bizarre aye-aye from Madagascar, have claws. Primates have large brains in relation to their body size, helping make them intelligent, good at problem-solving, and highly social (apart from the ones that aren't very social, like the orangutans). We primates also have a bunch of special adaptations in terms of our teeth and bones, which helps set us apart from other mammals. There are further splits separating strepsirrhines ('wet-nosed' primates) such as the bushbabies, lorises and of course lemurs, and our own family branch, the haplorhines ('dry-nosed' primates), which includes the bizarre but cool tarsiers, the monkeys and the apes.[13] With a few more twists and turns, we find ourselves further along the primate family tree until, at last, we come to the chimpanzees. They are found in rainforest and savannah habitats in sub-Saharan Africa; in twenty different countries, from Tanzania and Uganda in the east to Sierra Leone and Liberia in the west. They are what we call sexually dimorphic, which basically means the males and females look different from one another. Many mammals look the same regardless of their sex but

---

12 The spider monkeys' thumbless hook hands are great for swinging but they are rubbish for grooming family and friends. Grooming has such important social benefits that they've had to be creative in finding a replacement and instead cuddle each other to make friends and maintain relationships within their groups. All together now, awwwwwww!

13 This primate classification (or taxonomy) is both interesting and confusing. I could fill a whole book with it and there would still be arguments. The take-home message is that a tarsier from Indonesia (which just so happens to look like a gremlin) is more related to you than it is to a lemur such as the aye-aye from Madagascar. Have you seen a tarsier? Taxonomy is weird.

A king in the making. While only small now, young Max shows all the confident hallmarks of an alpha male (apart from size, strength and experience).

some, such as lions (think about the manes on the males), are different from one another. Chimps show a difference in size, with males being as much as 25 per cent larger than the females. Usually, males weigh around 60kg, which is about the same as a pretty big dog, but females weigh a little less, at around 45kg. Adult chimps don't really have any natural predators (I'm not counting humans here just yet) but they are wary around leopards, which, having lived near lots of wild leopards, seems a very sensible life choice to me.

While some primates have specific diets and eat only a handful of different things, chimpanzees are like me at a free buffet – happy to take a bit of almost anything. Mostly, they eat fruit, which accounts for around 75 per cent of their diet, but they also eat a range of leaves, seeds and bark. But don't be mistaken, chimpanzees are certainly not the model for new-age vegans or even vegetarians, as they supplement their mostly frugivorous diet with insects, small reptiles and birds and, in many instances, larger mammals. Some of my most life-changing animal encounters have centred around chimpanzees sitting down to eat. It reminds me of something that happened when I lived in Uganda, over a decade ago now. Every time the rains started, the forest floor would come alive for a day or two with flying ants and termites. All the big, fat, protein-rich ants would leave their underground fortresses to fly off and start new colonies. But the forest animals would be waiting. I have a happy memory of some colourful hornbills, young chimps and humans gathering these tasty treats from different nests along a path one morning.[14] Hunts were always big news and several times my team and I would watch in fascinated silence as the chimps would gather around us and scour the trees for the large and loud black-and-white colobus monkeys, or down on the forest floor for the dainty antelope-like duikers. There was a memorable occasion when I was with Joshua, one of the very best chimpanzee field assistants I've ever had the pleasure of meeting, let alone working with, in the forest. We were habituating the wild chimps, which helps eco-tourism, law enforcement, community initiatives and ultimately, conservation efforts. To habituate chimps, you basically need to get them to think you're the least interesting thing on the planet and to ignore you completely. It's easier said than done and takes months or sometimes years. Over time, the chimps go from fear (running away from you) to anger (running towards you) before finally coming to a point where they seem to realise that you're not a threat and, in fact, you're not even interesting to look at but you're annoyingly following them every day. So they may as well let you follow them, so they can get on with their daily business. This is when all the invaluable behavioural

14 If you're wondering, they can be eaten raw or cooked into an ant or termite omelette with some fresh chillies and onions. And no, they do not taste like chicken. They taste like popcorn, of course. In fact, when I finally left the forest for the last time, my farewell meal was a lovely termite omelette.

data can be collected, because you're close enough to see what's going on but you're not influencing their actions. It's a pretty special thing to achieve. Joshua and I were in the process of this habituation and were at the point where they were no longer freaking out because of us, but flipping between being angry and fascinated by us about a million times a day. It was late morning and we were deep in the south end of the forest. I was busy thinking about lunch[15] and it seems the chimps were thinking about roughly the same thing. It was Joshua who first excitedly whispered that he thought the chimps had gone rather suspiciously silent, which might mean they were thinking about a hunt. Over the next few minutes, we saw numerous little black and hairy faces peering down from the canopy or shadowy bodies passing along the pathways around us. I quietly suggested that they must have a poor little duiker on the menu, because they were all close to the ground. I can vividly recall Joshua saying how unnatural it seemed to have that many chimps nearby but suddenly silent. I even started feeling sorry for the duiker, but also morbidly lucky that it must be close and that we were going to get a front row seat[16] for what was about to be a raw and dramatic event. Joshua suddenly started speaking and was animated, so I 'shh'ed him… I know, don't say it. The little dark faces were closer now and I still hadn't seen the luckless duiker. Okay, it finally dawned on me that there wasn't a duiker nearby[17] and when I whispered this to Joshua, it was obvious from his expression that he was *way* ahead of me. We didn't have to battle for our lives and I'm proud to say that I didn't run and leave my slower colleague

---

15 Lunch was usually a mug of sickly sweet black tea from a very old flask, with a cold chapatti and jam. Don't let anyone ever tell you that fieldwork isn't glamorous.

16 If you're sitting there right now thinking 'what an idiot' then all I can say is that you can read chimps far better than I could back then.

17 Any self-respecting duiker would have been miles away, telling his mates about the two idiot humans in the forest.

Peek a boo. Like every young ape (including us), Max loves playing endless games.

to face an unknown number of hungry chimps. We just stood up. It was weird. It was almost as if we were suddenly all very awkward and a little embarrassed. The chimps moved off, we laughed nervously and had another cup of tea to settle our nerves and neither we nor the chimps ever mentioned it again. I still don't know whether it was a case of monumental mistaken identity or whether they were actually trying their luck. Either way, the point I am trying to make here is that chimps have a very varied diet. Despite all odds, we lived to habituate another day, which meant I was ultimately able to end up on the other side of Africa, with the Desmonds and their orphans.

# GOING, GOING, GONE?

Chimpanzees
and
habitat destruction

A shrinking world. Like many species,
chimpanzees are losing their homes through
various types of habitat destruction.

Gloria is little, eyes lowered to the ground, thin arms draped by her sides. She is silent and still, her breathing shallow and rapid, poised for what is about to come. The inevitable happens. In a flurry of leaves, Gola bursts over the plastic drum lying on the ground of the enclosure, hitting it loudly with her tiny feet, racing towards her friend. Abandoning the idea of a quiet moment in the dappled morning light, Gloria's eyes light up when she sees Gola and the two tumble over one another, laughing, pulling hair and playing. Little Gloria dashes off in a game of chase that will no doubt end up with the whole horde of young chimps joining in. So goes her life. But things were not always like this and Gloria is a long, long way from home.

Born in Zwedru, an area in northern Liberia, Gloria spent the first few months of her life surrounded by lush forest, which covered the landscape in a glittering emerald canopy, where raucous calls of hornbills pierced the still morning air as tendrils of mist and soggy cloud wound their way up through the trees and into the dawn each day. It's an area that has been a haven for countless species for countless generations. A place which is being destroyed at a heartbreaking rate. Where the daily chorus of chimpanzee pant-hoots is drowned by the buzz of chainsaws, and the gentle whisper of the breeze chasing its way through the forest is being replaced with the ear-splitting, heart-rending cracks of giant, age-old trees snapping as they crash to the ground. Each leaves a vicious scar in this once beautiful green landscape. It was from here that little Gloria was taken one morning. As her forest home shrank day by day, more men came. Some to take the trees, others to take the animals who had nowhere left to go. Parted from her mother after she was shot, Gloria was one of the lucky ones. She was rescued when she was around a year and a half old by the Desmonds and did not face the traumas experienced by all too many chimpanzee orphans. She arrived with Jimmy and Jenny at Liberia Chimpanzee Rescue & Protection and

Although still a youngster, Gloria is perfectly happy climbing through the canopy.

settled in well. I asked Jenny what Gloria is like as a person.[1] She smiled and I got the sense that Gloria is special. I've spent time with Gloria and know she is a capable and independent chimp. Jenny's answer supported this: 'Gloria's smart and a good problem-solver. She does not anger quickly but is mischievous and playful.' Sounds like a right enigma, doesn't she? Jenny told me that she is a natural leader and heads a band of female troublemakers – Gola, Lei Lei and Rebecca. She's apparently also very well mannered, which is something almost unheard of in chimpanzees and something I have yet to see.[2]

I look at little Gloria and she's a paradox to me. I'm so pleased that she's under the protection of the Desmonds and has such a great bunch of other chimps around her but at the same time, she breaks my heart. She represents something so big and so destructive. Habitat destruction is the single greatest threat to chimpanzees and although I could have chosen almost any other orphan to show this, for some reason Gloria embodies all that comes with habitat loss and destruction. Many chimps live in what we call secondary forests[3] or cling on in areas that have already been heavily logged in beautiful, primary forest. A place that should have been safe. But nowhere is safe from the disastrous effects of habitat destruction, as it marches its way relentlessly across Africa and the rest of the tropics.

---

1 I know it sounds peculiar when you first hear them referred to like that but believe me, after ten minutes with the chimpanzee, you'll know why I see them as non-human 'people'.

2 I'm not saying I don't believe that she's well mannered, just that the first time we met, she shoved her finger so deep up my nose I thought she was in danger of tickling my brain. I don't know where you're from, but where I grew up, that would not be considered the height of etiquette.

3 If the forest has never been cut, we call it primary forest. If there has been any disturbance, such as logging, the forest which grows back is called secondary forest.

Once upon a time, a green belt of forested habitat stretched almost uninterrupted across the African continent. Hiding the equator, it linked the western coast to the east. It was home to possibly over a million chimpanzees. When was this far-off distant time? Just a hundred years ago. It may sound like long ago but it was around the time my grandfather was born. So, in only three human (and chimp) generations, this pristine forest has been commercially cut, burned, ploughed, bulldozed, logged and farmed, leaving in many places no evidence that forest was ever there. As you might imagine, this has had a devastating impact on species that called these forests home. A century ago, chimpanzees were found in twenty-five African countries but now, largely due to the destruction of their forest homes, we can draw a line through four of those countries. It is with great sadness that Benin, Togo, the Gambia and Burkina Faso can no longer say they are home to chimpanzees (not that chimps always pay attention to official borders). Across the rest of the range, chimpanzees have found their habitats more and more fragmented,[4] with the consequence that populations have become isolated from one another. It's possible you're thinking: 'So what, humans are quite fragmented and we too are often isolated. I hardly ever talk to my neighbours and I'm okay.' Well, it is very different. At worst, not talking to your neighbour might mean you miss out on the occasional Christmas card or asking them to feed your cat when you're away for the weekend. But for chimpanzees, living in isolated communities can have long-term and damaging effects. It's all to do with having a genetically healthy population and the effect of inbreeding can be catastrophic. For any healthy population to flourish, it needs to be able to depend on a healthy genetic pool. If the pool of genes is too small, then we see the effects of inbreeding: increases in certain diseases and conditions, decreases in fertility. With a reduction in genetic

---

4 As well as smaller, generally.

Doing what chimps do, Jack hangs out in a tree.

diversity, the whole concept of natural selection and the 'survival of the fittest' stops. If a disease or natural disaster wipes out a big chunk of the population, the genetic diversity means some of that population will have a better chance of survival and will be better suited at recovering. If they're pretty much the same because the population becomes too small from being isolated, then the diversity needed isn't there. As a result, that population is more vulnerable. To everything. So, a smaller overall population of chimps is bad, and fragmented populations of chimps are also bad. Although, as we shall see, there are multiple reasons for chimpanzee numbers dropping, habitat destruction is by far the most widespread and influential of these.

But why is there habitat destruction? Easy – trees are being cut down, right? Well yes, but it's not as simple as that. If we ask why the trees are being cut down, we uncover a problem so complicated that it looks like some unsolvable puzzle or maze.[5] In a way, it's an equal opportunities problem too. It's not simply a problem of 'poor people in poor countries using firewood'. Yes, that happens, but it's bigger than that. Logging in Africa provides funding for global terrorism and props up corrupt governments. Surprised yet? It also makes the chairs you sit on, the floor you walk on and the bed you sleep on. It helps power your mobile phone. Okay, now are you surprised? There are two very obvious questions here: how is this happening and what can be done to stop it?

The answer to how it's happening is easier, if sad, to answer. Africa has been exploited for hundreds of years. When you look at a map of Africa, never forget that for almost every country on this beautiful red continent, the borders were drawn by white Europeans. Before we turned up in the early 1500s, Africa would have been a merry mixture of tribes, self-governing regions and kingdoms. Then, we either took it by force, bribed or bought off those rulers, kings and tribes. European powers squabbled

---

5 Or maybe the puzzle within a maze. It is such a complicated issue.

and haggled among themselves: 'If you have this piece over here, Belgium, then we'll have this bit there. France can have the bit to the south.' We never asked what Africans wanted or needed. We saw the land, habitats, animals and people as opportunities. As resources. Resources that we could cut down, hunt, shoot, enslave and trade around the world.[6]

The effects of this one-sided relationship with Africa lasted for centuries and can still be seen today. Many of the political problems started long ago when some random European bloke, far off in some random European city, probably in a ridiculous-looking powdery wig, had a 'good idea'. Previously friendly tribes were told to kill each other and some cultural groups were told they were less important than others, that they were barely human, in fact. And it all contributed to the habitat destruction we see today. Often, overseas colonial rule meant we drew straight lines on a map, across places we never even visited, through cultures we never knew or tried to understand. We destroyed communities and ways of life we never knew existed. We plundered what we said was ours, but which was never ours. It's a legacy which has lasted and looking at Africa now, it's undeniable that as well as the historical clearance of forest habitat, it remains industriously encroached, logged, burned and lost. Never forget that this global habitat destruction we see today has historical roots but, more importantly, never forget that it is not restricted to the history books and is worse now than ever.

Okay, let's deal with the most obvious cause for loss of forest habitat first; there's a whole lot of wood in a forest.[7] In Europe, we'd done a pretty good job of turning trees into houses, furniture and paper for a few hundred years. So much so, in fact, that we needed to look further

---

6 It is estimated, for example, that between the 16th and 19th centuries, over 10 million enslaved Africans were snatched from across Africa to work, against their will, in the Caribbean, South America, North America and Europe.

7 Isn't it just great when an academic shows off that razor-sharp intelligence. 'See Mum, that PhD was totally worth it...'

Jack plays with a leaf.

afield for our woody needs. Not only did we find a load of wood from across Africa but we were in luck, because it appeared no one was using it.[8] Better still, some of this wood was of an exceptionally high quality

---

8 As long as you don't count the chimps, gorillas, monkeys, birds, reptiles, amphibians, invertebrates, plants, fungi, oh yeah and the indigenous human communities. Because they *were* all using those forests.

and before long, ironwood was being used for railway sleepers, mahogany for 'beautiful' flooring in grand homes and teak for fancy ornaments and decorations. Across West Africa alone, it is thought that around 90 per cent of the forest cover was lost across the last hundred years. Wouldn't it be nice if we could get to this bit of the book only to see that here's the part where I tell you it's all okay now? That we're in the twenty-first century and we finally saw the problems we were causing by cutting down the 'lungs of the Earth'. We saw how bad things were and came together as a global community to tackle climate change, habitat destruction and species extinction and that finally, it stopped. It would be lovely, wouldn't it?

It would also be wrong. Data from Global Forest Watch shows that we have not stopped, but we have intensified it and now the estimated area of tree cover loss, measured by satellite, between 2016 and 2017 for the African continent is in the region of 15,000 km$^2$. Of course, I'd be at fault if I didn't mention local, small-scale extraction. Communities do cut down a good chunk of the forest, mainly for building materials, or to clear for farming or for charcoal production. Charcoal is great for cooking because it burns hotter and longer compared to wood. However, it's terrible for forest conservation. I've seen how it's made and if you want to produce 1kg of charcoal, you will need to burn about 10kg of wood. You don't need to be a maths wiz to see the problem here. I'm sure research has been done into the overall impact of such community-led deforestation, but there's no escaping the fact that it is not on a local scale but on a commercial scale, both nationally and internationally, where we see the 'business end' of deforestation. From Kenya to Nigeria and from Mozambique to Madagascar,[9] Africa is losing her forests. Research has shown that a combination of five

9 Madagascar *is* a part of Africa, remember. It often seems that people forget this. Either way, there's a huge problem with deforestation and habitat destruction on this wonderful island, with its unique biodiversity.

main factors are largely responsible for global forest loss. Commodity-driven deforestation, shifts in agriculture, large-scale forestry, wildfires and urbanisation all drive habitat destruction, with different influences having a greater or lesser impact in various parts of the world. Broadly speaking, a shift in agricultural practices is behind much of the deforestation across Africa. Even looking at Liberia, the impact of commercial forest clearance is staggering. A single oil palm company has a government concession whereby 2,200km$^2$ of forest cover is

Hanging out. Rebecca laughs as she clambers through the trees.

To make sure they receive the proper nutrition, Gloria and the other babies are given a special formula several times a day.

allowed to be cleared over the next twenty years. Already, as well as quitting the Roundtable on Sustainable Palm Oil (RSPO), an internationally recognised eco-certification scheme, the company has razed several thousand hectares of forest to the ground, making way for the production of palm oil, which is cheap, easy to process and, as a result, found practically everywhere. It's used in our food, cosmetics, cleaning products and as fuel and may be in as many as half of the products we buy. Palm oil has already had a devastating impact on tropical forest habitats and species across parts of South East Asia and now appears to be doing the same in Africa.

We started this chapter, however, looking at little Gloria and how she ended up with the Desmonds and for her, at least, the worry is now over. Yes, she lost her forest home and for a while her future was far from certain, but now she spends her days with new friends, in the care of Jenny and her team. Gloria and her mates have a long and happy life ahead of them now but if Jimmy and Jenny are to give them the best life, they will need to provide them with another forest home, where they can run and swing and play and fight. Where they can forage for food and find shelter. But in the same way that these things would not necessarily come naturally to us, the Desmonds will have to teach their chimp orphans the skills they'll need to flourish in the wild. To achieve that, they'll need to develop a rather unusual school, where the lessons are unlike any other.

# WELCOME TO CHIMP SCHOOL

## Teaching apes to be wild

Wonderment. Lei Lei stares up,
observing the world around her.

Often, after discovering I'm a biologist (and especially after learning my first degree is in Animal Behaviour), I'm given a scenario and asked whether its result is 'nature or nurture'. 'Ben, my cat only likes salmon when I take the skin off and feed it to her on a fork. Is that nature or nurture?' If there's one way to make biologists puff out our cheeks and roll our eyes, it's asking us to psychoanalyse unhinged pets. But it does open an interesting can of worms. What makes us[1] do the things we do? Why do turtles and eels cross oceans to produce new generations? How does every Arctic tern know how to get from the North Pole to the South Pole that first time, every time? Does every orb spider hatch with a plan for the right design of her web or does she watch a grown-up spider do it first? The answer is staggeringly simple. It's complicated.

It's almost never the case of something being down to nature or nurture alone but a subtle, complex combination of the two. Trying to understand animal behaviour is one of the most wonderfully self-indulgent things in the world, similar to unravelling a giant ball of tangled wool using only your eyes! Fascinating but difficult and bloody frustrating. The simplified idea is that some behaviours are innate, or within us (the 'nature' part of the theory), while others are the products of learned behaviour (the 'nurture' part), either as a result of watching others around us or from being taught. My interest isn't how we separate behaviour into one or the other camp but, instead, taking a behaviour and dissecting it to reveal the influences of both nature *and* nurture and how they interact. Something I've wondered time and again while working around the world with so many members of that wonderfully bizarre family we call the animal kingdom is whether wild animals are truly born wild. It sounds like common sense but we take it for granted that being 'wild' (whatever that might mean) is somehow

---

1 By 'us', I mean humans, chimps, eagles, the manky-looking pigeons in your local park, cookie-cutter sharks, sarcastic fringeheads, nudibranchs, peanut worms and every other member of our extended animal family.

the behavioural baseline. Some things are obviously innate: the need to eat, sleep, drink. There's no question there – that's just biology happening. Gurgling stomach-centric stuff telling us we need more fuel or brain-based telegrams firing between synapses, telling the body that it's about to start dreaming, so it might as well do the right thing and start sleeping first. That's all physiology, right? But *how* does a chimpanzee know what to eat? *Why* do they build a nest each night, so that they might sleep safely? When I worked in Uganda, the chimps there ate over 220 different species of plants, from juicy ripe fruit and the slippery pith of inner bark to leaf after leaf after leaf. I'm not a botanist; I've tried but repeatedly failed. I can identify a mammal species from a single toe bone and can distinguish a colobus from a cercopithecine monkey from a cough, but I seem to have a botanical blind spot. I'm proud of myself if I can distinguish an oak tree from a daisy, but in a tropical jungle, where many plants look so similar and where, very often, a tasty leaf closely resembles one which will cause pain and death, I'm not sure I'd last more than a day or two. Add to this that different populations of chimpanzees across Africa eat different things, then it becomes clear that a certain amount of learning must be involved somewhere along the line. So, although the need to eat is fundamental to a chimpanzee, *what* a chimpanzee eats is fundamentally different. It needs to learn.

It came as a revelation to me that even though many animals (not including chickens, hamsters, puppies and other species we've spent millennia domesticating and making have floppier ears, bigger eyes and nicer temperaments) are born actually being wild, they're not born knowing how to *be* wild.[2] Here's where cultural learning (or cultural

---

2 All you really need for this is to be born in the jungle, on a coral reef or within the Arctic tundra. If someone lovingly wraps you in a blanket, places you in a basket or sticks a photo of you on social media within the first few seconds of life, you're probably not all that wild.

Petrol head. Max demonstrates why it's important to provide proper enrichment activities for the inquisitive, unruly kids.

transmission) comes in, and chimpanzees, along with a few other intellectual champions such as crows and their relatives, dolphins and some monkeys, are experts. Cutting through the science, this means that many social species are reliant on the learning and passing on of information within groups and down generations. It means that culture (for this is what it is) is seen across the animal kingdom. It also means that human beings are not the only species to demonstrate a set of rich cultural traditions and that we cannot use the presence of culture to define our bizarre little species. Everyone from scientists and philosophers to religious scholars has had a good go at defining what it means to be a human being and has tried everything from tool use to culture to justify why we are the most special species on the planet. Spoiler alert: we're not.

For young chimpanzees growing up in the wild, life is one big classroom and every day, every encounter, every activity is a lesson from which they can learn. They, like us, learn through a combination of techniques, namely experience, participation, imitation, communication and innovation. Through these, a young chimpanzee might be able to tap into this cultural learning stuff for himself or herself, where success comes from passing on learned skills and information within a group. Chimps are good at this mode of learning because the adults invest a lot of time and effort interacting with one another and passing that down to their young. Imagine the alternative: having really awesome but complex behaviour is no use if every generation has to reinvent the wheel,[3] so to speak. These cultural behaviours, which we sometimes term as *traditions*, are not passed down genetically, that's the important thing to remember. When this was investigated by scientists in the late 1990s and early 2000s, they found that when taught a new trick within a group, the same behaviour often ended up in another, neighbouring group. They also found that, like humans, chimps appear to prefer to learn from older members of the group, rather than younger 'experts'. Think about it: on the whole, don't you tend to feel happier learning from someone who appears to have gravitas, experience and has successfully made it around the block a few times without too many bruises or missing digits?[4] Finally, and I'm not sure how I feel about this, but again, like us, chimps are subject to peer pressure, meaning that once something is established within a group, we see behavioural conformity. So it's unlikely that a young chimp in the wild will be using a hollow reed to suck out termites, rather than fishing for them, any time soon.

So, why have you just sat through a lecture on cultural learning and transmission among non-human apes? First, because you find inherent joy in discovering the answers to some of life's bigger questions and more interesting phenomena. Also, because I wanted to show how

---

3 And sometimes quite literally.

4 The only exception to this is with new technology, maybe. I hate to generalise but I'd rather rely on any playschool-based expert over my parents, for example. Maybe it will be the same when chimps invent their version of the iPad, although it'd presumably be called an aPe-ad.*
* I'm not even sorry.

heavily young chimps rely on their family and other group members to acquire the skills they'll need. It's essential. Now imagine what effect ripping an infant away has. Those baby chimps taken from their mothers, destined for the pet trade but which thankfully end up in a sanctuary such as the LCRP, are turning up with none of the skills needed to survive in the wild. It's something we need to focus on when thinking about sanctuaries and the animals they house, but it is a big problem as, as well as taking care of the veterinary needs and psychological requirements, the wild needs of sanctuary animals should be covered. Here's where *chimp school* comes in. Yes, you read that correctly: chimp school. Let me say now that no, it's not like Hogwarts but with hairier pupils and no, there's no detention, essays or maths homework. There are however, lessons, there is lots of group work and there are exams.

You're still imagining a classroom full of hairy little students sitting in boisterous rows at ancient desks, aren't you? I can tell. Deftly made paper aeroplanes gliding from the back of the room and Bui looking innocent, maybe. Star with her hand up, correctly answering with an 'ook',[5] a smug look on her innocent face. Stop it.

In reality, sanctuary schools where young apes are rehabilitated are fairly common. I've seen it with orangutans in Asia and chimps in Africa. I'm not sure if it happens as much with gorillas, as gorillas are like a foreign language to me... I wouldn't even hazard a guess. They're a funny bunch and it could go either way. Sanctuaries are busy and overstretched but they do what they can, where they can. I'd been lucky enough to do a few learning-based activities during my time in Uganda but I have since been much luckier in West Africa. From the start, the Desmonds told me they were putting a lot of focus on making sure

---

5 I know for a fact that chimpanzees don't make this sound but an author far greater than I has already set the precedent for anthropomorphised great ape expressions. Who am I to argue with the late, great Sir Terry Pratchett?

their orphans were going to do lots of these activities. Chimp school activities serve two main purposes, each as important as the other. They provide enrichment, which is of huge importance. Although enrichment is basically the idea of keeping an animal in captivity occupied or 'busy', I can't emphasise enough how much this is needed if you are to stand any chance of having a group of happy, well-rounded animals in your care. As a rule, the more intelligent a species is, the greater the potential for problems in captivity. They develop stereotypies, which are any number of behaviours, specific to a species or type of animal. They can be hard to define but from the perspective of a scientific definition, stereotypies are abnormal repetitive behaviours, which usually arise as a result of being in captivity without the opportunity to express a normal range of behaviours. These negative behaviours serve no function or role for the animal and show very little variation between individuals. For example, bears rock continuously, horses bite the bars of their enclosure, big cats pace in circles. Often endlessly. I've seen tigers do this so much in some bad zoos[6] that they wear down the grass in their enclosure, through constant pacing. Primates are equally prone to stereotypic behaviours, which range from repetitive pacing, swinging and swaying to pulling out their own hair, excessively scratching one area and even constant face-pulling. It's not always obvious that the behaviour is stereotypic but once you're attuned, you'll notice how common such abnormal behaviours are. The problem isn't always in the behaviour itself. Pacing, for example, isn't a bad thing necessarily, but stereotypies are an indicator of something bigger (and worse) beneath the surface. That old comparison to an iceberg is done to death, but it's true for stereotypic behaviours. You might only be able to see a small part on the surface but, like the

---

6 And sometimes, in some good zoos too. These behaviours are very quick to appear, very hard to remove and an indication of how hard it is to care for animals in captivity.

proverbial iceberg, most of it is hidden from view and that's where the real danger lies. To reduce behavioural problems, it's vital to provide enrichment. This can take almost any form, from complex feeding games to throwing food on the ground rather than providing it in a bowl, so that the animal must forage to find it. Enrichment can be using ropes for swinging, balls and slides for playing, pools for bathing, you get the picture. Almost anything that prevents boredom and encourages more natural behaviour.

The other role of chimp school[7] is that it is a good opportunity to teach the orphans some of the key skills they'll need if they are to have any chance of life in the wild at some point. A big conservation goal for many sanctuaries is that, one day, the animals being cared for might be returned to the wild, benefitting not only their welfare but contributing to the survival of the species itself. It's not always possible, either due to habitat destruction, the risk of sanctuary animals introducing diseases (as a result of contact with humans) to wild populations, or simply because we can't guarantee their safety.

There is a wonderfully strange example of why it is so important to provide animals with the skills needed to be wild. An example which covers enrichment and 'wild lessons'. This example is monkey school: 'golden lion tamarin school', to be precise. These enigmatic South American monkeys are as beautiful as they are rare. But we very nearly lost them in the mid 1960s. Usual stuff – loss of habitat and overhunting took their toll and the tamarins teetered on the edge of extinction. What followed was one of the most successful captive breeding and reproduction programmes ever, where nearly 150 zoos[8]

---

7 Or orangutan school, gorilla school, elephant school, parrot school, etc. These school programmes are practised in sanctuaries around the world, for a range of species.

8 While it's no big secret (or surprise, probably) that I'm not a massive zoo fan, they really can contribute to conservation in lots of positive ways, including conservation education and 'real world' conservation action such as this.

Bath time. Even a tub of warm, soapy water provides the kids with enrichment and helps them strengthen social bonds.

around the world, and countless conservationists, field assistants, researchers and zookeepers, ensured this magical-looking monkey stayed out of the history books. But this success story came with a few hitches. After a bunch of monkeys had been raised in captivity, matured and given the all-clear veterinary checks, they were released into the forest, where they were monitored, while the conservation world waited with baited breath. But disaster struck when they started falling out of the trees. A frantic rescue mission saw them safely collected and taken back into care. Heads were scratched as the team investigated. Some suggested that an obscure neurological condition they might have picked up in the wild could be to blame. The answer was much simpler. In captivity, the tamarins had been taught how to feed and to distinguish tasty from toxic foods, they had learned about predators and been given all the key skills they'd need. Apart from one. They'd never walked on bouncy branches before. Their enclosures had food, water, shelter and hefty metal or wooden beams across which they could move around. But when they were released into the wild, all they had were those rubbish, bouncy, flexible, *natural* branches which are surprisingly common in a tropical forest. Having never experienced walking across real branches, they just couldn't get used to them. Some fell from the canopy. Others chose to move through the forest at ground level, which is not ideal when there are terrestrial predators, such as lots and lots of ocelots. After a quick refresher course, where they could learn how to overcome those troublesome trees, they were once again released, and now there are healthy populations of wild golden lion tamarins once again. It might be tempting to see this as a massive oversight, but that would be wrong. It was a pioneering project and so many of us have learned so much from it. It demonstrates how important it is to teach captive animals as many 'wild' behaviours as possible, regardless of how obvious or natural they may seem. After all, what could be more natural than a monkey bouncing around in a tree?

Back with Jimmy and Jenny, we looked at introducing the kids to a range of lessons, some more for enrichment, others for necessary 'life skills'. We conspired together and it was a lot of fun designing which games and lessons to introduce. As an ex-teacher and a current university professor, I'm used to creating courses and lectures, but this was the only time one of my lessons included a cargo net, a concrete termite mound, rubber snakes, and jars and jars of honey.

The key to success is class size. None of this twenty to thirty students in a class, or fifty to a hundred undergraduates. Optimal class size at chimp school is four or five. Maybe six if they are an even remotely well-behaved bunch, or if you're feeling especially energetic and full of caffeine. Any more than that and you're running around after the ones who would rather go and catch a butterfly, or who really need to climb

Social climber. Providing the sleeping quarters with ropes makes it a little more like the forest for Lucy.

Aping around. Like the other kids, Poppy finds even the simplest task hilarious.

a tree right now.[9] Some games or lessons are just too simple for many of the kids and it's not cool to climb a cargo net when you're already happy to drop from overhanging branches, swing perilously on ropes and cannonball off the climbing frame into the side of my head while I'm looking the other way. Yes, I'm looking at you, Jojo. Again. I remember feeling a sense of disappointment when none of the kids appreciated Jimmy and me hauling a very heavy cargo net into what, to me at least, looked like an awesome afternoon activity. They ambled over to it, sized it up, walked off. Brats.[10]

My faith in near-humanity was however, restored when Ella had a go. She had not been in long and was still finding her bearings. She's one of my favourites, even though you're not meant to have favourites (human or otherwise), but there you go, I'm a fickle, biased biologist. Ella was tough and independent and wouldn't stand for any messing from her new foster-brothers and sisters. Being just a year or so old, she should've been nervous and uncomfortable leaving Jenny, her surrogate mum. At this age, wild chimps cling on to Mum for dear life and only venture a few steps away. Instead, Ella stomped over, grabbed the bristly netting and hauled her scrawny body up, tiny muscles flexing and bunching as she turned and twisted, pirouetting in front of us and turning upside down. She laughed. It was a moment of sheer joy for me. Here she was, this little ape, barely big enough to climb herself, playing and dangling with reckless abandon. This victim of the bushmeat trade, who had been dragged from the forest, dressed in baby clothes and offered for sale at a busy city crossroads before being rescued, was happy again. Gaining confidence, developing life skills

---

9 Or, more realistically, breaking up endless squabbles.

10 I am more than used to human students looking at me with that 'this is lame' expression etched on their faces but it's even worse when a non-human primate gives you that very same look.

and benefitting from the enrichment of this new game, Ella excelled at her first taste of chimp school. Over the next several months, I worked with Jimmy and Jenny to introduce new skills to the younger kids through various chimp school ideas. One day, Jimmy and I demonstrated that, despite having five or six university degrees between us, we really could not make a 50cm-high fake termite mound out of cement. After several hours, our hill resembled a school project volcano, but with lots of holes replacing the crater. We left a gap in the back where a jar of honey could be placed and inserted thin sticks and stems in the holes to give the kids a head start. Termite fishing is a well-known behaviour, seen in many wild chimpanzee populations across their natural range. Termites and ants are a good source of protein. Young chimps learn from older group members (via that cultural transmission stuff) how to select the right tool, such as a long, thin but strong grass stem, and how to insert it into a crevice. Next, they pull it out and drag it across their mouth, eating the tasty invertebrate morsels, which have bitten into the stem (as they try to defend their home), before they have a chance to sink their sharp, piercing mandibles[11] into inquisitive fingers or lips. Some of the orphans were intrigued and watched, some were natural termite hunters and set about with razor-sharp focus, and some realised there was a gap at the back, where naughty fingers could dip straight into the honey jar. All perfect responses,[12] in terms of innovation, imitation and cultural learning.

The cargo net lesson was heart-warming. The termite (aka honey) fishing sort of went to plan, but everyone agreed that they'd had fun, regardless. The other activities, such as nest-building and nut-cracking, were roaring successes. Each served to enrich the kids, develop and

---

11 Insects don't have teeth, they have mandibles. They still hurt as much when digging into your finger, though.

12 Despite the sudden unintentional rise in sugar rushes.

Concentration face. As he tries to figure out the 'termite mound', Bui, like many of us appears to stick his tongue out to focus.

reinforce confidence and social bonds, and taught them some of the fundamental skills they'll need in the wild, or at the very least, when they are in a more natural situation, after the sanctuary moves to the forested mangrove peninsula nearby. Of course, the kids haven't learned everything there is to know about each activity. At best, they've served as tasters. Some of these skills take years and years to perfect. Nut-cracking, for example, is the most difficult skill a wild chimpanzee will ever learn. I had never seen it during my time in Uganda with the eastern subspecies of chimps, as it has only ever been documented in western and central African populations. It was something I'd always wanted to see for myself. Taking the right 'anvil' stone and finding a 'hammer' stone, a chimp can crack open the hard shells of seeds and nuts within the forest. Sounds easy and, to be honest, it looks pretty easy too, but it can take up to eight years to get it right. If you still think it sounds simple, try cracking a walnut against a brick, using a rock from the garden or beach, and let me know how you get on. You'll either smash the nut to tiny pieces, hit your thumb hard, or cause the nut to turn into a ballistic missile as it rockets away from your *expert* attempts. Or, probably, all three. It goes to show that we should never look at something like intelligence from our perspective alone.

My favourite chimp school activity though, and the one I think was the most important, was the day we did the forest version of *stranger danger*. Growing up is always a stressful and possibly dangerous period for any young social ape, us included.[13] A big challenge for inquisitive and adventurous little chimpanzees is that, in a forest, danger is never far away. One of the biggest threats is which of the other forest inhabitants are harmless and which are deadly. These could be predators, or animals which defend themselves with lethal consequences. In a word, snakes. You may not want to see them, and you may not

---

13 Or us especially, maybe.

actually come across them often, but the average tropical forest is full of snakes, of all shapes and sizes.[14] Some are harmless,[15] but some are venomous and pose a threat. Some are so venomous that a single bite can kill humans (or chimps). The last thing we would ever want is to save a chimpanzee orphan from a horrible life in captivity, equip him or her with confidence, and then watch that confident kid go and play with a Gaboon viper, green mamba or spitting cobra.

I'm going to introduce a bit of a disclaimer here. This next bit, on the face of it, might seem wrong. I intentionally introduced stress to animals whose brief lives were already packed full of stressful memories. You might ask whether it's fair to scare these vulnerable orphans and maybe you'll disagree, but my answer is yes, in a situation such as this, I believe it's necessary. If five or ten scary minutes can help ensure these precious lives are safer, then I'd argue it's justified until I'm blue in the face. So, although the 'snakes' lesson might seem funny,[16] or may appear mean or even unethical, it was done to make sure the kids would know what to do if and when they encounter a snake in the wild.

With snakes, it has to be an 'all or nothing' approach. It isn't possible to teach the kids how to distinguish a harmless green tree snake from a boomslang, or a rat snake from a rhinoceros viper. The plan wasn't to train simian herpetologists, but to make sure the kids survived what could be a deadly encounter. If we got to the point where 'snake equals bad', then the lesson would be a success. Jenny and I planned to run the lesson with two groups. First of all, the 'littlies', who would never have encountered a snake, and then with some of the bigger kids, who

---

14 Admittedly, long and thin is a common serpentine blueprint among the group but there is still a lot of variation in how long and how thin.

15 In fact, most are harmless and want nothing to do with you at all, although I'm not sure how true the old adage 'They're more scared of you than you are of them' is.

16 It *was* funny, I can't lie.

might already have seen snakes, either in the wild or since having arrived at the sanctuary, as snakes are often seen around the enclosure where the older kids are housed. In the Desmonds' compound, there's a beautiful old tree. I've no idea what species it is – definitely not an oak. The thick grizzled trunk meets the earth in a chaotic explosion of roots, which stretch along the ground in every direction. Fallen leaves gather against the root buttresses and the innumerable twists and loops make this ideal snake habitat. Jenny and I sat among the roots, busy ants scurrying over us obliviously, the shade of the canopy offering welcome relief from the midday sun. Just the sort of place young chimps might play in the wild. With us were Max and Bui, Poppy and Ella, all playing happily. Unbeknown to them, I had already hidden two rubber snakes in the root tangle. One was much larger than the other, one pale, one dark. As Jenny and I chatted, we discussed the role of nature and nurture in identifying predators and even which of the young ones would perform better in this 'life and death' situation. Time and again, a chimp would unsuspectingly get very close to one of the snakes. Each time, we both held our breath in anticipation. Just how inherent self-preservation was in primates with regard to these long slithery things was something we were about to find out. Max was by far the most confident within this little band. He has a hilarious swagger, which gives no hint of his diminutive size or his lack of 'alpha-hood'. Maybe one day he will lead the others, but for now, he was our best hope. Would he throw a stick at the snake? Would he alarm call to warn his friends of the imminent danger? What would he do?

Finally, our star pupil noticed the snake, the big one. He silently walked over, slow and cautious. All his focus was on this new thing. And then all his focus was on grabbing the snake, sticking it into his mouth and gleefully sucking on its tail, or maybe its head. He had no idea which. By some twist of luck, the snake coiled around Max as he turned away and he couldn't have looked happier, snake draped over

Stranger danger. This rubber snake was used to teach a valuable lesson to the kids, making them ready for a life in the forest.

him, tail (or head) in mouth, unaware of danger. The crazy kid was even laughing. As much as we chuckled, Max had failed and, had he been in the wild, he would now be dying as neurotoxins coursed through his frail body. So we did what any caring adult chimpanzees would do and taught him a lesson, urgent and fast. It's hard to phonetically write down exactly what a chimp alarm call sounds like, but on paper it would be a loud, high-pitched 'wa-hoo'. The impact of our calls was instant. Fear broke out. Chaos reigned.

The fun new toy wrapped around Max turned into the focus of everything that was suddenly bad and wrong. To say that Max went ape is a fair assessment. As he flailed and 'wa-hoo'ed, running to Jenny (and the other kids) only served to scare the others. The snake snagged on a root, Max escaped and jumped into Jenny's waiting arms. Bui, who had sensibly climbed a tree to escape the snake (and the snake-entangled Max), now wanted a cuddle too, and started wailing. Two things struck me. First, how instantaneous the response was when we sounded the alarm call, but also (unlike the others?) how little baby Ella cared. She barely responded to the fuss and only kicked off when she felt that those precious Jenny cuddles were being shared around too much. Jenny and I aggressively called out at the snake, so that the slithery bastard got the message not to mess with any ape in the future. We even threw sticks, so the kids really got the message. I used a branch to flick the snake away and we were finally all safe. There was lots of cooing and whimpering, which I assume is the chimp equivalent of reliving a moderately scary incident to your mates, with suitable exaggerations and embellishments. After everything calmed down a while later and the incident was a distant memory from at least twenty minutes ago, Bui happened to come across the other, smaller snake. It became plain very quickly that a single encounter with the snake was all it took to have an impact. Madness erupted again.

As I said, the snake lesson may, on the surface, seem harsh, but that stressful situation could mean the difference between life and death for these kids, so I reckon it's wholly worth it. Some of these lessons are for fun and some teach physical coordination or develop cognitive skills. Others however, save lives. This is the beauty of chimp school. These orphans have already been through so much, often surviving unimaginable conditions and experiences and, as ever, those of us who are fortunate enough to play even the slightest role in their lives should do all we can to help ensure they are as wild as they can be. After all, they are not pets, are they?

# SO CUTE...
# I WANT ONE!

Chimpanzees
and the
pet trade

Although it is so easy to see how people find these
babies cute, the illegal pet trade is wiping out wild
populations of chimpanzees.

Let me set the scene. You have a pet chimpanzee and she's beautiful. Her deep brown eyes are playful and alert. She loves it when you groom her and she could spend hours lying there, letting you sort your way through her coat, picking imaginary bugs and beasties from between the long black hair. Occasionally, she purses her lips gently against your fingers as you allow her to 'inspect' these existentially dubious parasites. Her favourite snack is a juicy ripe banana[1] and she loves nothing more than a cuddle, stroking your face tenderly as she looks into your eyes. You dearly love your pet chimpanzee.

Now, let me interrupt this moment between you and your pet and ask you how old this imaginary pet chimp is. I'm 90 per cent certain that this cute friend of yours is a baby chimp, maybe a couple of years old, at best. Not very big at all. Am I right? Why is it that most people won't visualise an adult female chimp in this idyllic scenario? Because you'd have to be an absolute idiot to do this with a mature ape and there's every chance an adult pet chimpanzee will one day attack you and at best, bite off your fingers. At worst, she'll simply tear your face off or kill you in a seemingly unprovoked attack, hallmarked as much by its speed as its ferocity. I am not trying to scare you away from chimpanzees as a species or necessarily paint them in a bad light in general, but I am trying to scare you off the idea of ever thinking a *pet* chimpanzee (or any other primate, for that matter) might be a good idea. Because it's really, really not.

When I first went to Liberia, I had that exhilarating thrill of meeting a new group of strangers. Some human, but mostly I'm referring to the new bunch of chimpanzees I met for the first time. Those lucky enough to be in the care and have the love of the Desmonds. When I show friends and family photos of the kids, and there are a lot of photos, and yes, this happens way more often than can be deemed normal, I'm

---

1 She's nothing if not a cliché.

often asked how I recognise the different chimps and how I learn who's who. My standard answer is something like, 'Well, it's the same as when you have a new class of students and they all look the same at the start,[2] but after a week or two, you notice the differences and eventually learn their names. It's just like that, really.' For the most part, that's true, but what I don't say is that I find it so much easier to identify individual chimps than I do my students. I'm not entirely sure what that says about me and chimps, or my students, for that matter, but the point is that, like us, chimps look different from one another. I often wonder how far this applies through field biology. I know gorilla researchers look at unique nose prints[3] and scientists studying humpback whales use the colour, pattern and shape of the tail and fins to pick out individuals, but what about pandas or penguins? They really do look the same to my untrained eye and I can only imagine that zebra researchers out on the savannah use barcode readers to tell Fred from Freida within the herd. Once we are able to identify different individuals, we are able to form the foundation of a bond with that individual and as social apes ourselves, this is what it's all about – forming attachments throughout our lives. Given that we're hard-wired to seek out, form and maintain social relationships and considering that baby primates like chimps look so undeniably cute and that they 'act just like us' anyway,[4] it's not a huge shock that primates have been considered perfect pets and have been kept around palaces, houses or apartments for years. There are records dating back millennia of pet

---

2 Big sorry to my students, past, present and future, but it's true. You do all kind of look the same at the start. And if you think that's bad, the next bit will really upset you.

3 Yes, this is the clearest and quickest way to distinguish gorillas. Each one is as unique as a fingerprint, apparently.

4 Never mind that it's us who act just like them, really.

monkeys and even now, despite our increased understanding of their welfare, husbandry needs and safety requirements, there remains what seems a never-ending supply of naive or ignorant people who not only look at a primate and say, 'Aww, I want one' but who go right ahead and actually get one.

In terms of easily distinguishable chimpanzees and the topic of keeping primates as pets, Sweetpea is the sad but perfect example for me. She is one of the oldest and largest of the chimps currently being cared for by Jimmy and Jenny and among the first I was able to identify there. In fact, way before I set foot in Liberia, Jenny used to send me countless snaps of the babies and kids and Sweetpea always stood out. When I met her, I felt as though I knew her instantly. I think she has the most relaxed face I have ever seen in a chimp and is like one of those wonderful people we occasionally encounter who does yoga every day, meditates and is worry-free, stress-free and calm. In a stormy and

Happy face. The lovely Sweetpea shows a huge chimp smile.

turbulent world, dear Sweetpea is a shining cloud sailing carelessly through a tempestuous sky. She has the most soulful eyes, and can genuinely usually be found smiling or laughing. A chimp smile is wonderfully distinctive. The upper teeth are covered by the top lip and the lower teeth are left exposed, with the mouth hanging open. She has thick tufts of hair on either cheek and the skin around her eyes is dark, making it look as though she's wearing a mask. There's no denying she's one beautiful and friendly chimp. She is one of the only larger ones who (now I am much more experienced with what is and isn't safe to do with chimps) I am comfortable enough to groom through the mesh of the enclosure and to allow to do the same to me. Although I also love Portia, for example, who is the same size and age as Sweetpea, she wouldn't hesitate in giving me a quick slap, hair tug or worse, given half the chance. But Sweetpea is different. She comes up to the mesh, greets me excitedly, reassuring me by lifting the back of her hand towards my face. This is a classic chimp-chimp greeting and only the most devious and wilfully deceptive chimp would do this and then behave badly immediately after. Portia does just that, by the way.[5] After Sweetpea has greeted me, I can take her wrist and inspect the hair on the back of her hand, to check for dirt and critters that I can remove. She loves it (and so do I) and it's never long before she's showing me her feet to groom, turning around so I can inspect her neck and check her ears. She positively disappears into some sort of simian heaven if I take a tiny stick and run it gently under her grubby nails, showing what's accumulated beneath, real or otherwise, before yes, pretending to eat it myself. I think Sweetpea reminds me of Pasa a little, so it was probably inevitable that I would fall for her. What's worse is that she is similar to Pasa in another way, in that she doesn't seem to associate herself with the other chimps around her and is, it seems, perpetually trying to seek

---

5 Can you begin to see why I might love her a little too?

Growing up. As one of the oldest orphans, Guey will become harder to care for as she gets bigger.

out human contact. I'll admit it: the idea of having Sweetpea living in my home alongside me has flitted through my mind on a number of occasions and has made me smile. She's so gentle, she doesn't even seem to like half the other chimps, she'd be much happier living with m… and then it's gone in an instant. Such thoughts are ripples across an otherwise tranquil lake, fading as quickly as they appeared. Because as lovely and as gentle as Sweetpea is, I would never want her as a pet. I could never provide the social contact she receives from her own kind, even if they are sometimes annoying and devious. I can't give her the space or freedom she'd need and you cannot reprimand a wild animal when she breaks a treasured ornament, ruins your new curtains or tears up your favourite books, page by page.

Primates are not domestic animals. We have been habituating, taming, domesticating and breeding animals as pets for thousands and thousands of years. The domestication of the humble hamster started in the early 1800s, transforming them from wild and wily rodents to the loveable full-cheeked scamps we know today. Domestic cats have been on a longer, 9,000-year journey with us, turning from haughty, demanding and aloof felines in the wild to, well... haughty, demanding and aloof felines in our homes, where they sit on our sofas and sleep on our beds. Dogs are the showcase of domestication, though, and we now believe the transition from wolf to what would ultimately become a prize-winning sausage dog may have started as long ago as 36,000 years. Lots of other animals, from horses, rabbits and even goldfish have been domesticated to make them suitable as pets, a process which not only physically changes the animal but often includes major behavioural alterations. Whether you think it's right or wrong to keep a pet dog, for example, there's a big difference between having a puppy that is the product of over 30,000 years of selective breeding and a monkey or ape that was either born in the wild or is only one or two generations out of the wild. A pet primate is still too inherently wild, has too much going on in its head to be able to adapt to living alongside us as a pet. There's also the ethical issue of whether we have the right to keep another thinking, feeling, sentient primate as a pet, when they are in fact capable of many (if not all) of the behavioural and emotional attributes we like to think separate us from our non-human kin. Finally, primates are very different from cats and dogs, horses and hamsters in that they require an extraordinarily high level of expert specialist care to ensure their physical and emotional needs are properly met. Psychological problems among primate pets are rife. And awful physical conditions such as warped and twisted skeletons resulting from metabolic bone disease caused by the wrong food or the wrong housing (or most likely both) are far too common. It's hard enough for a zoo to keep a healthy population of primates, let alone someone who, although they may have the best intentions, simply doesn't have the time, money or expertise to care for them properly. If you keep a monkey or ape in captivity and you keep it incorrectly, then you can expect things to go really wrong really quickly. If they're young, then rickets can develop, or if the problem starts later in life, osteomalacia can be seen in adults. Both these conditions affect the skeleton and bones become warped, eroded and fragile. Even the surface of the bones changes from the hard, smooth material it should be to become brittle and pitted. In some poor individuals, it becomes so bad that you can actually poke your finger through the bone of the skull. It's terrible, but often you'll have no idea the animal even has a problem until it's too late. I know primate sanctuaries in the UK full of ex pets, where animals with pitifully twisted bodies can finally receive the care they need.

I hope you noticed that? Where I said that these animals are in sanctuaries in the UK. They're here and in the US. They're in France, Germany, Spain, Italy. They're in China, Japan, across the Middle East and throughout much of the 'developed' world because, again, this is a problem which is not limited to South and Central America, Africa and across South East Asia. It's easy to see a problem such as this from a culturally elitist perspective, where it's probably 'all down to poor people in those poor countries and that with a bit of education or a few good prison sentences, the problem would go away'. But it's not that simple and the primate pet trade is thriving wherever you are. Admittedly, people aren't keeping gorillas as pets in London or Paris, and chimpanzees and orangutans aren't as commonly kept as monkeys and their prosimian relatives such as lorises, but from my perspective at least, it's all the same. Primates are not pets; they do not make good pets and keeping them as pets supports, and in many ways drives, their extinction in the wild. Having worked throughout Africa and in South East Asia within primate conservation, I've seen my fair share of monkeys kept as pets and chimps in sanctuaries and orangutans in rehab programmes, but I can remember the shock I felt when I discovered that there are an estimated 4,500 privately owned primates in the UK alone. That's right, there are thousands of them here somewhere and what's worse, it's currently legal. I'm not talking about apes or any of the larger monkeys such as mandrills or baboons, but there are numerous species which can be bought, sold, bred and kept. I had never met anyone who owned primates in the UK and had never even heard of anyone keeping them, but a quick search online showed how easy it is to purchase a whole range of South American species. I was writing an article on the problem of primates as pets for a national newspaper and had heard that, due to the negative image associated with keeping them as pets, primate owners were infamously secretive (cagey, you might even say) and didn't openly advertise what they were doing. Then, out of the blue one day, a young woman emailed to see whether I could help with a situation involving a small group of primates she had ended up with. Although there are some horrific examples of what can go wrong when keeping primates as pets,[6] this example encapsulated the problem for me. Laura[7] wanted to make sure she did something that would help alleviate the problem of people keeping primates as pets. From what she said to me, it was evident she could see that it required a huge amount of effort and specialist care to

---

6 Many of us know about the tragic incident that occurred in the US in 2009. Travis was a 13-year-old male chimp, living in a home in Connecticut. He was already famous and had appeared on TV shows and even in a famous fizzy drinks advert. As he got older, though, he became more difficult to control and was prescribed a well-known antidepressant, a human drug used to treat anxiety. After escaping from his house one day, he attacked the lady who lived next door. Something had snapped in this 'normally happy' chimp and he ripped off her hands, nose, lips, eyes and even the bone from her face. Miraculously, she survived but with life-changing injuries, despite since having a full facial transplant. Travis was shot dead by police and the world got a reminder of how dangerous pet primates are.

7 Of course, this isn't her real name. I changed it because, despite not wanting people to keep primates as pets, there's no point in publicly attacking someone who is ultimately trying to help these animals.

look after monkeys. It was also evident that while she recognised that most people who owned primates weren't up to the task, Laura believed she would be able to help. So she trawled through internet adverts for monkeys she could try to rescue and finally spotted the perfect thing. The ad was from a man in the Cotswolds who was finding caring for two common marmosets extremely difficult.

She contacted the man and agreed to collect the two adult monkeys – one male and one female. They had been kept in a tiny shed in his garden and she told me that when she arrived, they were in a terrible condition. He'd fed them almost entirely on porridge, baby food and fish fingers. When she asked if he had given them any fruit or vegetables, he remembered that he'd occasionally fed them grapes. Neither monkey had ever been seen by a vet. 'The male had severe dental problems and his tail was a mixture of matted hair and bald patches.' Like so many of us (me included), Laura had grown up fascinated by monkeys and other primates, and although she had never intended to keep primates, she found herself rescuing these two South American monkeys. She realised that the female was pregnant and, two weeks later, twin males were born. Soon after, the adult male from the original pair was booked in for surgery to fix his tail and teeth. While he was under anaesthetic, the vet discovered that his body was riddled with metabolic bone disease caused by poor nutrition and insufficient light. Sadly, the male died during the operation – though, with his twisted bones and body bloated by gas, it seemed a blessing when his heart finally stopped. This cheerless story doesn't stop. Before he died, he'd managed to get the female pregnant again – and soon another three tiny males were born. Laura then rescued another adult male (this time from Luton), and what had started out as a single pair now turned into a family of seven – with the new male acting as a surrogate father.

I heard from Laura about a year later and the update wasn't what I especially wanted to hear but neither was it surprising. Some of the monkeys had to be separated because of fighting, one of the twins had mysteriously died and there seemed to be ongoing difficulties with how to successfully mix members of this extended family without either fatalities or unwanted pregnancies. It struck me that as much as she had tried to do the right thing, Laura was on a very steep learning curve with these animals and ultimately, they paid the price. Now, she was trying to provide the best possible care for rescued animals and was keen to seek advice from experts; but Laura in no way represents the average primate pet owner, in terms of her knowledge and desire to seek help from so many experts. Even the average vet is not fully able to deal with primates when things go wrong, as they require specialist care and treatment. As far as I know, Laura's rescue family is still going. The last I heard, she had provided them with a specially made enclosure, specialist heating, specific lighting, indoor and outdoor runs and an ever-changing regime of feeding and behavioural enrichment. Contraceptive implants ensured no more surprises have arrived on the scene and now, finally, both the monkeys and keeper are as happy as they can be.

It was insightful speaking with Laura. Not only because it highlighted how hard it is to care for primates and how quickly things can escalate from bad to worse, but because she was so honest in what it was actually like to keep primates. Openly admitting that primates make awful pets, she told me they urinate on everything to mark their territory and smell terribly; they need constant care and easily cost thousands of pounds every year to keep. 'People have this idea that they can touch and cuddle them, but I never touch mine as they're not tame,' she said. 'If I did, I'd expect to be bitten. Even with my most relaxed animal, I wouldn't dream of it as it would stress him out too much. It's such a selfish thing to have them as pets. Get a dog, anything – just don't get a monkey!' Well, there's the endorsement of the century. Primates suck as pets.

One small step for Bui, one giant leap for chimpkind.

I'd tried contacting several other primate owners but, with this one exception, none would speak to me. I sense that they know it is wrong at some level and would be uncomfortable talking about it. Of those 4,500 primates kept privately as pets in the UK, while some are owned by trained experts and represent specialist breeding groups, the vast majority are pets, living in people's homes. Often owned by individuals with nothing more than good intentions and the misguided desire to own a 'cool' pet, I suspect there are few privately owned captive primates in such a fortunate situation as those Laura rescued.

I wanted to explore how different it is to keep primates as pets compared to those housed in zoos. Are we being too tough on pet owners, maybe? I asked a friend who would know better than almost anyone what the issues are in keeping primates privately. Dr Sharon Redrobe is a veterinary surgeon and the Chief Executive Officer of Twycross Zoo in the UK and knows first-hand how hard primate husbandry is. 'By definition, a pet is an animal we touch and play with in our homes and in no way is it in a primate's best interest to be constantly touched and played with by people,' she said. 'They need their own social groups, are extremely hard to care for and often grow up to be aggressive and impossible to control. Owners then take them to a vet, expecting them to be magically "fixed". They're wild animals and, in that respect, no different to tigers. You wouldn't keep a tiger at home, so don't keep a monkey.' Sharon is however, quick to point out that in the past, keeping pet primates was far more socially acceptable and that places such as Twycross were actually founded by people who liked to keep pet monkeys themselves, but she says times have moved on. 'The world has changed hugely since the 1950s and 60s. We didn't know any better then; now we do. If you really love monkeys, let them be monkeys.'

So, if those who own primates can see how problematic they are and experts who specialise in primate welfare think it's a bad idea, then how is it okay to keep them in somewhere like the UK? Despite such complicated care needs, high welfare concerns and the serious risks associated with the spread of certain diseases between people and non-human primates, it is still legal to keep primates as pets in the UK – regardless of how endangered they are or how dangerous they may be. The care of primates is covered by the Animal Welfare Act of 2006 and the 2010 Code of Practice for the Welfare of Privately Kept Non-Human Primates (the 'primate code') set out by the Department for Environment, Food and Rural Affairs (or DEFRA for short). The act, which states that animal owners must prevent 'unnecessary suffering' and must take 'all reasonable steps to meet their animal's needs', is hard to enforce as there's no need to register ownership of many primate species and, in any case, most pet primates in the UK are kept in secret. What's more, the primate code is primarily intended to explain the welfare and management needs of the animals and to breach it is not actually an offence – though it could be used as evidence in court in animal welfare cases. The code, which applies to everything from gorillas to lemurs, is further weakened as it is subject to broad interpretation and specific groups of primates are not covered in any significant detail. The keeping of some primate species, such as capuchins, is thankfully restricted under the Dangerous Wild Animals Act (1976), but many, including marmosets, are not listed. A 2014 report by the Royal Society for the Prevention of Cruelty to Animals (RSPCA) found that over 80 per cent of pet primates in the UK belonged to the marmoset group, originally from South America. However, we really have no idea what's going on because when the last report was published, based on local authority applications to own primates, the results (Figure 1) showed that lemurs were 'officially' the most commonly kept primate in the UK, with capuchins the second most common and then macaques. Bizarrely, marmosets don't even feature, as the registration of marmosets, tamarins or squirrel monkeys isn't thought to be necessary here. In looking at results from when the RSPCA is involved in a call-out or investigation centring on a primate, however, marmosets account for over 45 per cent of the issues. It shows that we have no accurate data of which primates are being kept and how many there are, or a means to systematically record that. To say the law needs to be updated is an understatement.

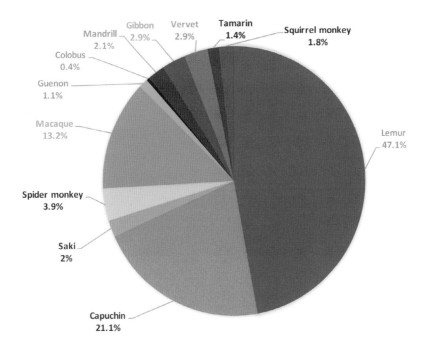

**Figure 1.** This pie chart is based on an RSPCA report compiled from applications people made under the Dangerous Wild Animals Act in order for them to own a primate. Although you are supposed to register primates in this way in the UK, most people don't and not all primates, such as marmosets, tamarins and squirrel monkeys, even need a licence. To help see where these animals come from, the African and Madagascan primates are labelled in blue, the South American monkeys are in red and the Asian primates are in green.

Key strategic groups – including the Primate Society of Great Britain, the RSPCA, the British Veterinary Association, the British and Irish Association of Zoos and Aquariums (BIAZA), which monitors and regulates zoos in terms of husbandry and captive care, and the international animal welfare charity Four Paws – support a ban on pet primates and are gathering evidence and data for a government review, hoping that one day, it will be illegal to own a primate pet within the UK.

The primate pet trade is part of a huge global problem. Each year, hundreds of millions of animals are traded live internationally. In the US, the Centers for Disease Control and Prevention, the government agency at the front line in identifying, recording and tackling new diseases and outbreaks of known diseases, estimates that, annually, an average of 350 million fish, 640,000 reptiles, 4 million birds and around 40,000 primates are traded, bought or sold from one part of the world to another. These numbers include the import and export of food, supply of animals to research laboratories, and the pet trade. It's a problem which is growing. Welfare groups in the US such as the Captive Wild Animal Protection Coalition (CWAPC) believe that a new trend whereby primates are considered as replacements for children, or a status symbol for celebrities, is causing more people to seek a pet primate. I can't decide which of those is worse: the need for some sort of surrogate where someone obviously needs to love and be loved, or the vapid desire of careless celebs, vainly seeking new ways to look cool, different or stylishly nonconformist. On second thoughts, I do know; whereas I actually feel something for the former, these 'inspiring' celebrities are setting a bad example for millions of fans. Even in the last few years, some of the most well-known and biggest names in music have all been snapped either with pet monkeys, or have used primates during a performance. The only positive side to the stupidity is when they fall foul of the law. In 2013, one celeb was given a capuchin monkey for his birthday. He thought it was a great idea[8] to take the monkey from the US to Germany on tour but was surprised when German customs officials confiscated Mally, the monkey. Rather than sort paperwork, the monkey was abandoned and fortunately rehomed in a zoo where, even years later, he is said to be suffering from psychological problems. Even within the US, another musician landed in hot water for keeping a young capuchin, which he bought as a Christmas present. After posting videos and photos online, he was charged with illegally keeping a primate without a permit.[9] Monkeys such as these, and other primates, form part of a trade in live animals worth $10 billion a year. Around 90 per cent of those wild animals destined for the pet trade won't survive their first two years in captivity.

Behind all the depressingly impressive stats and despite problems such as being taken too early from their mothers, the effects of social isolation and often cramped caging, we need not to lose sight of the individuals behind the numbers. Sweetpea was the first chimpanzee to arrive at the Desmonds, along with Guey. She was taken from a Chinese restaurant in Liberia, where she was half pet, half public curiosity. From what little I know, she hasn't got a history of being beaten and she doesn't show any obvious signs of psychological trauma, but here's the thing: she does have a legacy from her time as a pet. She doesn't have to have some sort of horror story background for this to be a miserable tale. There are plenty of pet chimps kept by well-meaning and loving owners, but the reality is that this is a life sentence. For every single primate. For each chimpanzee. For Sweetpea.

---

8 You even know what I'm going to say here. It wasn't a great idea, it was a steaming pile of stupid. Imagine being so vain that you think international laws don't apply to you.

9 If any pet primate owner is going to get in trouble with the law, it has maximum impact when that person has millions of followers and fans, so it gives me a warm fuzzy glow when I hear a celebrity owner has received a visit from the police.

All alone. Ella, and every other orphan, was taken from her family. Only the lucky ones end up in sanctuaries.

Chimpanzees live for a very long time. Gregoire lived out his days in the Tchimpounga sanctuary in the Democratic Republic of the Congo, after spending forty years alone in a zoo. He died as Africa's oldest chimp, at sixty-six. One US safari park says that their oldest chimp resident, Little Mama, died at the almost unbelievable age of seventy-nine. Whether they can survive into the late seventies or not, pet chimpanzees like Sweetpea have decades ahead of them in an environment other than their forest home, living a life a long way from what should have been. Even those lucky few, like Sweetpea, who end up with the incredible care she receives from the Desmonds, still have a very, very long life ahead of them. It is so bittersweet seeing her, knowing she is safe now but also knowing she will never be truly wild because of one person's desire for a 'cute and cuddly pet monkey'.

If there's one thing I would like to see in the next few years, it would be for the US and the UK to make it illegal to own a primate as a pet. It's wrong. We know it's wrong, and it would be such an easy win for politicians. Already, fifteen European countries have introduced bans on keeping primates as pets, either for all or some species. Let's hope we can increase this number and let wild chimps, orangutans, gorillas, monkeys, lorises and lemurs remain wild. Every chimpanzee in every African sanctuary has two things in common. The first is that they are there because of the illegal pet trade. Worth a few hundred dollars locally but up to $20,000 on the international market, and glorified by the ignorant actions of films, advertising companies and celebrities, there is regrettably still very much a demand not only for chimps but a whole host of primate species within the primate pet trade.

The other thing that sanctuary chimps have in common? While they were all destined for the pet trade, they are all orphans and have lost their mothers and closest family members to a far worse trade: the bushmeat trade. But that comes later, because before we look at this awful exploitation, it's important to remember that chimps from every background, whether as a result of habitat destruction, the pet trade or bushmeat, must first make it to the sanctuary if their story is to be told.

# GOING IN ALL GUNS BLAZING

Following a chimpanzee confiscation

Sanctuaries are full of orphaned chimps. Each has a tragic story, detailing the transition from wild animal to shackled prisoner, before finding the refuge of the sanctuary. One of the most wonderful things about working with chimpanzees is their individuality, and the frequency with which something about them is unique: each face, each personality. Every like, dislike, preference and tantrum is unique to that particular chimp, just as it is with us. Another thing unique to each orphan is how they arrive in a sanctuary. You never know when to expect one. They range from almost newborn to mature adult. Some are calm, some are sociable. Others may lash out in fear. Some are handed in by their owners, either because they're worried about getting into trouble or because that cute little fluff-ball has transformed into an aggressive, stressed out, unmanageable wild animal. Some, however, are confiscated and this is a double-edged sword. It's a sign that partnerships between the local police, forestry department, wildlife sanctuary, conservation charities and even government are on the same page. It's the sort of thing I talk to my students about when I want to give a good example of 'successfully collaborating stakeholders'. The flip side of a chimpanzee confiscation is that it is a traumatic experience (for every species of ape involved) and, like so many things about a chimp, is different each time. I want to take you on a chimpanzee confiscation, letting you see it through my eyes, as it occurs. You'll get a glimpse of the stress a chimp must endure and of the love and commitment shown by those such as Jenny, who dedicate their lives to saving these precious beings.

Like so many dodgy stories, it begins in a car park, outside a run-down hotel in the midday African sun, with a plan being made over the bonnet of a car.

It's so, so hot. Unbearable. It's the tail end of the rainy season, the only relief from the sweltering heat is the almost intolerable humidity. I am with Jenny and a team of Liberian sanctuary staff, formulating a plan for the hours ahead. The grass is thick and coarse and scratches my ankles. It looks more blue than green, the sort found throughout the tropics and definitely not for sitting on to enjoy picnics. Although I'm listening to what's being discussed, there's an old-fashioned razor blade lying in the grass which, for some reason, I am fixated by. I think, more than anything, it's a way for me not to really concentrate on the task ahead. We're on the outskirts of Monrovia, waiting to join an armed international police task force as they raid the property of a suspected wildlife trafficker. I've been in plenty of surreal and threatening situations as a biologist, but the most dangerous are always those involving people.

There is a plan, I'm assured, but I get the distinct impression that it's more of a loose idea than a militarily precise schedule. The police are to go in first. There's some talk that the people we're off to see[1] might be 'entrepreneurial' and rather than limiting themselves to wildlife trafficking, they might have expanded their horizons into other lucrative activities such as the drug trade and even arms dealing. Our job is to go in after the police have done their bit securing the site, in terms of the human side of things. When it's much safer, hopefully. It is quickly apparent that, in terms of today, the word 'safe' is up for interpretation. First, we have no idea how many chimps there might be. There could be one, there could be a bunch. They could be babies, which, from a practical point of view, would be easy to look after. They could be juveniles, who will be much harder to secure, handle and safely transport back to the sanctuary. As long as it's not an adult, then we're fine. Rescuing an adult chimpanzee would be an absolute nightmare. The second area of safety uncertainty[2] is that 'there may be

---

1 Sounds almost sociable, doesn't it? Almost jolly. We weren't really off to 'see' them – we were off to do a surprise raid, make some arrests and confiscate some chimps.

2 This sounds like a thundering understatement in this instance…

cobras'. Oh right. I'm not scared of snakes and I'm not scared of cobras in particular. I love them too. I used to have a big wild cobra which lived close to my little forest home in Uganda for a few months and often used to see him or her[3] in the mornings. I may even have warmly greeted my herpetological neighbour when the cabin fever got especially bad. What I don't love is that there's a chance these cobras (if there are any) might be released during the raid. It would be a guaranteed way to keep the police at bay and would give the bad guys time to escape. I can't help but visualise a room full of shouting, armed cops lined up against a wall, fleeing criminals and a swathe of cobras, up and hooded, threateningly swaying as we curiously peep around the open doorway. That safety plan we discussed is already hurtling off piste but hey, there are chimps to confiscate. We wait. In the thoroughly uninspiring car park, under the merciless mid-morning sun, the rusty razor blade winks at me as it catches the light. The raid is nearby. They've obviously not told us where so that the traffickers have no chance of finding out what's in store. I wonder who exactly it is in our team the police suspect will run and squeal to the bad guys.

The call comes – Jenny is talking to one of the officers on the phone. The conversation doesn't last long, and we pile into our vehicles, eager to be on our way. It turns out that the raid is not close by but a good twenty or thirty minutes away. There's an air of tension in the car I'm in. Everyone seems to be awash with nervous excitement. The team we're working with is an international wing of a law-enforcement agency, so important people across Liberia will no doubt be watching how today goes. If it works, Jenny will be a step closer to helping to develop a dynamic team from different agencies and charities who can

---

3 While I love cobras, I'd never get that close. I'm silly but not stupid. When people want to know what the difference is between being intelligent and smart, I like to think it's intelligent knowing how to sex a cobra. It's smart deciding not to go ahead and actually do it.

tackle wildlife trafficking here in Liberia. If we fail, all that is at risk. No pressure then. But thoughts of politics and armed criminals and even cobras fade as I, like everyone around me, constantly think of the chimps who need to be saved. We're driving through endless neighbourhoods, each looking slightly less affluent than the last. Houses are shabbier, roads have more holes than tarmac, something in the air is telling me this part of town isn't as friendly as some of the others might be. When I was growing up, my mum and dad ran pubs and I was taught to be alert always. I am good at reading a crowd. I don't know how many times that's been invaluable in my work as a conservationist, and probably even when habituating chimps, but my warning bells are starting to jangle about now. One of the team receives a call and we're to collect the senior police officer somewhere up ahead. It has to be quick, as he has officers in the area who he doesn't want to be seen with, so that they're not targeted in revenge attacks by the local community in the future. Yes, it's that sort of neighbourhood. We pull over and he opens the door, letting hot and humid fuggy African air rush into the cool, air-conditioned car, reminding us again just how hot it is outside. The officer gets in. There are awkwardly cramped handshakes, greetings, and explaining who's who. He's a big guy, dressed in dark jeans and jacket over a blue T-shirt and out-of-place, immaculately white trainers. I was expecting a police uniform, or at least an official-looking armband or something. The only clue is a beaded metal chain disappearing under his T-shirt, which holds his hidden police badge. I realise that we are not off to rendezvous with a squad of uniformed, armed cops, but a mixed team of officers, dressed in their own clothes, who are going to do what they can today. It's the sort of thing that would never happen in the UK or the US, but even after all this time, I sometimes forget and my western expectations are almost superimposed over the reality before me. This is one of the poorest countries in the world. The police are doing the very best they can but there is no trained squad, there isn't a police car today. No one has a gun. In fact, there aren't even any handcuffs.

Things don't go to plan. For whatever reason, they can't find the compound we're planning to raid. There's a mix-up with road names and locations, or something. So the police haven't gone in and it's decided it will be easier if we all go together. That small, sensible voice[4] in my head is telling me to wait it out. That I don't know what we're going into and that, in all honesty, none of this feels safe. But there is that other part, that voice which makes me swim with tiger sharks or walk through the dark house at night to investigate a mysterious noise I hope is the cat. The voice that makes me stand far too close to the precarious edge of the Great Rift Valley, which is winning. It tells me to get out of the car now.

The officer is quietly spoken and seems a haven of calm among the frenetic energy in the car. I know I'm stressed, and Jenny is too, in a way I've not seen before. She's put so much into coordinating today, forging ahead with agreements and cutting through red tape to create an alliance, so that this might become a regular thing, and criminal gangs might think twice before trafficking wild chimps. Today needs to go well. No mistakes.

I'm not sure how best to describe the area where we stop. The terms 'neighbourhood' or 'suburb' seem totally wrong, but so does 'slum'. It's 'rough'; that's as precise as I can be. We turn off the main road and bump along a deeply rutted dirt track, miles from the centre of the city now. The police officer is on his phone again, quiet but authoritative. He points ahead, along the road, to where a skinny guy in a bright red shirt is waiting. He sticks out like a giraffe at a mongoose party, but apparently he's another undercover police officer, who has been trying to find the compound. We park next to

---

4 Yes, I do have one, and yes, it is very, very, very quiet, usually.

him. He tells us the trail has gone cold because, although they know the compound is within this block, there's no info to help narrow the search. Everyone is getting out of their vehicles. More police in plain clothes appear. We talk about what to do next, hoping this is not all for nothing. Then, we hear it. The faint but distinct call of a young chimpanzee in distress. The timing is unimaginably perfect. Jenny and I look at each other, almost checking to see if we both heard the same thing. Jenny quietens the group and we hear it again. There's no doubt. There is a little chimp here somewhere and it's in trouble. Everything happens quickly now. Our biggest fear is that whoever has the chimp has heard about the raid and, to avoid trouble, releases or, worse, kills the noisy kid to avoid it leading the police to their door. We run through yards and around houses; as harrowing as the calls are, there's still hope for as long as we can hear them. Endless scenarios are racing through my mind. What's the striking range of a cobra? Where's the best place to hide if shooting starts? How long can a tourniquet be applied for? What if it's a *spitting* cobra?

There is no compound. No criminal masterminds. No guns. No cobras, spitting or otherwise. But there is a chimp. We are in the middle of a cluster of single-storey homes. Ramshackle places made from large, poorly fired bricks, covered with crumbling white plaster. A clothes line stretched between two homes, with bright garments hanging lifelessly in the sun, separates the yard. A radio is on; two women sit on plastic stools, washing more clothes. They look up and if they're surprised at the sudden appearance of what seems like half the Liberian police force and some random white people in their yard, then they do a very good job of hiding it. There is a naked human child. I am rubbish at ageing little humans – somewhere between one and three years old, that's my closest guess. Probably closer to the former. With chimps, I can tell much more accurately, but human kids are alien to me. He's carrying a length of wood, which he trails through the dusty ground, making a shallow path with its tip. Next to him is the chimp. She looks to be around two years old, maybe a tad younger. She's alive.

In these first few seconds, I'm scanning so many things at once, assessing everything I can. She seems relatively calm, no signs of malnourishment. She's a good size. She's a she. She has a nasty dry skin condition, but that will clean up soon enough, with the right care. There's a chain round her neck tethering her to a large rock in the yard. It's not a heavy chain, thankfully. The chain is attached by a material collar around her neck. It doesn't look too tight, but it's worn the hair away there. I can see she has teeth, meaning they've not been removed. She's using all her limbs and there's no sign of injury. Her eyes are bright and alert. They follow the tip of that stick the child is holding everywhere.[5]

Men turn up, asking us who we are and what we want, and disappear upon discovering the police are here and they're looking to arrest someone today. The brother of the guy who owns the house arrives. Tells us that there were two young chimps but that one 'had to go back because he was bad'. Jenny tries to find out what this means but it's confusing. We have no idea whether the other chimp has been sold, killed or dumped in a forest patch somewhere. All we can do is focus on the one here. Jenny and I roll the large rock and she pulls the chain free. She asks whether the chimp has a name. One of the women, who was washing but is now watching the circus performance, tells us that this little girl is called Star. It's a beautiful name for a beautiful little kid. I don't know why, but instantly I like the name. It suits her. The guy who owns both the house and Star turns up. There are a few people with him.

Some greet Star; she reaches up gingerly with a little clenched fist at the end of her outstretched arm. They 'fist bump' her in response, to

---

5 Sometimes, it's what you can't see that you need to look at the hardest.

I know you were expecting world-class glossy photos, but some of these were taken on a phone, in stressful and sometimes dangerous situations. I'm not a great photo snapper at the best of times. I thought you'd like them anyway, to really see what these situations are like.

Prisoners. Star was rescued from a yard, chained by the neck to a rock.

The face of fear. After being beaten for years, this adult male is terrified of his owner.

howls of laughter, and what seems a genuine sign of affection for Star is actually a depressing sight of an orphaned little ape, a long way from home and her dead family, surrounded by people who just don't know her language, even the basics. My attention is drawn back to the humans. Jenny is asking whether the chimp is for sale. 'Of course she is,' replies the guy and goes into some sort of mad self-haggle, giddy at the thought that this random white woman might be the perfect buyer, despite being surrounded by cops. A price is agreed[6] and the police take over now. It's hardly a coup in undercover police work, yet he still manages to look shocked and affronted as the officer explains that it is illegal to keep and sell a wild animal and that as well as Star being confiscated, he's off for a visit to the police station back in town. He turns angry and argues back. One of the officers grabs his wrist and suddenly the fist-bumping crowd of happy spectators is angry too and are being vocal about it. An angry crowd has the potential to turn into a terribly dangerous beast. It thinks, moves and acts as one, not rationalising but responding on impulse. It takes one voice from the bank to shout 'Get him', or one stone to be thrown, and the floodgates open. That's my fear. Two officers drag the guy off. I get Jenny and Star away, around the side of the house out of sight of the crowd. We have a police officer with us and I'm heading back to the cars. Another man walks up to us, says he's police. Tells us there's another chimp nearby, in a different compound. Says that the people there might kill this second chimp if we don't act now, as news of the police arrest is spreading through the neighbourhood. Also, casually mentions that this new chimp 'is a big one, by the way'. Erm, what?!

We have Star. She clings to Jenny. The confiscation has gone well. It isn't the international gang of wildlife crooks we heard it might be, but regardless, an arrest has been made and a chimp has been confiscated.

---

6 I genuinely don't know what he was thinking.

Stunted. Fed a diet of alcohol and scraps, this adult male is much smaller than he should be.

Innocence lost. Shortly after being rescued, Star settles into life at the sanctuary.

Bonus points for no cobras. But here we are, running between buildings again, the group split up, following a guy who I don't know is definitely with the police. [7]

As we run through the fierce African sun, some kids wave and smile at us, others start to cry. Two old men sitting on a step look up at us, one with an expression of contempt. I wonder what we must look like to this community. Undercover cops and outsiders carrying a baby chimp, streaming through their usually quiet streets. We get to a large compound. Thick white walls surround it, maybe a couple of metres in height. There are already a lot of people around the metal doorway. They're expecting us. A new police officer joins us here. He's a dominant guy, with a broad smile that doesn't hide his tough character very well. I sure as hell wouldn't want to mess with him and I'm glad he's with us. He reassures us that he has called for armed and uniformed officers, as the situation may be unsafe. Then we go in anyway. That back-up never arrives. Living quarters take up two of the inner walls of the compound. In the yard, people, livestock and a bunch of dogs are milling around, doing their thing. There are a few trees and some old, functionally extinct cars and a flat-bed lorry, loaded with decrepit crates and covered by tattered, worn sheeting. Our group walks towards the houses but I squat low to scan between and underneath the vehicles, desperate to find this big chimp before it's too late. I spot movement. It's an adult chimp. Things just got a whole lot more dangerous.

He is chained by the neck to a tree and is sitting on the ground. He hollers at the sight of our group bursting into the compound. It's a holler hard to describe unless you've heard it before, like the raucous wail of a pantomime dame, trailing off into loud, gurgling stops and starts. It sounds like a terrible imitation by a man who has never heard

---

7 I have to admit at this point that I trust no one and suspect everyone. It's probably because I was a teacher.

a primate in distress before, but is giving it a go nevertheless. It's a sound I've heard in the wild when an adult chimpanzee is being attacked or aggressively picked on by another, bigger chimp. A sound designed and tailored to be as pitiful as possible, in order to elicit the aggressor to stop. It's a male, we can see that. As we get closer, he gives us a massive, scared fear grin and wails again. Broken bottles of cheap alcohol surround him and there's a long, thin cane lying out of his reach. The booze is there to subdue him when he's being noisy and the stick for the beatings when the drink won't shut him up.

Confiscating any chimp is dangerous. You don't know their temperament, or what they've been through. Will they respond by attacking you out of fear, or jump into your arms, gratefully? Do they have a disease which could be passed on to you if they bite or scratch you? There are many unknowns and here we are, a couple of metres away from this scared, aggressive, very strong male chimpanzee. What scares me most is that even shooting an attacking chimp won't always stop them, not that we have guns anyway, remember. Here's hoping everything calms down soon.

Although he's got a sizeable set of teeth and an adult-sized head, he is much smaller than he should be – years of malnutrition have taken their toll. Jenny asks how old he is and the guy who says he's the owner[8] tells us this chimp is about thirteen years old. This piece of news hits me hard. I've been working with chimps for thirteen years and the thought that he's been here, chained to that tree, abused and beaten that whole time, infuriates me and although I'm not a violent person, in that moment I want to grab that long flexible cane myself. Jenny asks what his name is. It's the same as my younger brother's, and my anger gives way to heartache.

---

8 This is refuted later when we're at the police station. It's amazing how 'possession is nine-tenths of the law' changes when the law says that possession is, in this instance, illegal in the first place.

Suddenly the chimp lunges at Jenny and me, completely unaware that we want to help him. Stronger than both of us put together and fuelled by fear, he's as dangerous as a lion right now. He screams, exposing large canines, his steel-hard arms rushing towards us, partly to push us away, I feel. We manage to release him from the tree with no one hurt (badly), before managing to secure him in one of the vehicles. Throughout the rest of the confiscation, some things go wrong and others go right. In among the activity and noise and confusion, we leave the compound in a convoy, safely carrying humans and chimps alike. As we drive back to the police station, I'm with Jenny and one of her team, Star and two police officers in the back of the car. The stress of the last few hours runs its course and we laugh and joke as we relive the craziness of the day's events. As we go over some of the especially absurd moments, one of the officers turns to me and asks where we're off to. Somewhat confused, I tell him that we're going to the police station, obviously. Surely, he should know, right? Little alarm bells start to ring when he replies 'Oh, okay. What for?' That high-level stress begins trickling back to somewhere deep into my nervous system; my amygdala is probably doing frantic somersaults at this point. Jenny catches my eye in the rear-view mirror and asks the two 'officers' what they do for a living. One says he works in construction, the other simply mumbles incoherently. Great.

'You're not police, are you?' I ask.

'No, we are not police,' says the professional mumbler.

'Then… why are you in this vehicle? Who told you to get in with us?' I feel as though I need to ask, for the sake of clarity, if nothing else.

'The big police officer. He told us to get into this car.'

'Of course he did. Perfect. So, tell me all about construction work in central Liberia for the next twenty minutes or so, would you? Leave nothing out. Please.'

As brave and headstrong as ever, Jenny locks the doors, so they can't escape. As for me, I am looking for the quickest way out now ready for when they realise where they're going and why. It's around now that I feel this police force definitely needs to invest in a few pairs of handcuffs at the very least. I may even make a donation.

It all ends well. Little Star and the adult male both end up safe and sound at Jimmy and Jenny's place, admittedly with the aid of a cup of fruit juice mixed with ketamine for the big guy. Chains are removed, and they settle in well over the next few days. I never found out what happened to Star's owner, while I was at the police station and my two back-seat companions were being charged. I think he may have evaded justice this time. This confiscation was in no way normal as far as these things go, but to be fair, it wasn't especially abnormal either. Plans go out of the window, there's always a huge element of the unknown and the chance that something dangerous might happen. No two confiscations are the same, the only real thread that links them being that you do it because you know an orphaned ape needs saving and because you know that this one day might be the first of a much better, happier life for them.

# HAVING THE FAMILY FOR DINNER

## Chimpanzees and the bushmeat trade

Would you eat this person?

What's the most exotic thing you've ever eaten? It's a question which sometimes crops up when travellers[1] get together and end up comparing notes. It's a slightly geekier version of that scene from *Jaws* where the two doomed guys on a doomed boat compare scratches, bites and scars. I'm a fully fledged vegetarian now but have eaten my fair share of the natural world and I guess my two most outlandish meals were dried-out sea cucumber gonads in Madagascar[2] and termite omelettes in Uganda. My team (me included) used to love the flying ant and termite seasons, when countless insects would emerge from their underground homes before flying off to try and start new colonies. We sometimes even used to take half a day off to collect them as a tasty seasonal treat. We used to fry them with garlic and chilli, mix in a few eggs and voilà – a very nice meal. And before you start wondering, they taste just like popcorn. Honestly, they really do. When I left my project, my last meal was a spicy termite omelette, and I wouldn't have had it any other way. But there are countless people around the world who eat things which many of us would consider peculiar or wrong.[3] We're used to eating sheep, but does the thought of eating a goat feel slightly odd, for some reason? While many will happily tuck into a steak made from a cow, the idea of a horse being slaughtered, butchered and seasoned with salt and pepper before being served feels very different. You might not want to eat rabbits, but plenty of people do, and as for guinea pigs… well, even they're not safe from the cooking pot. It depends on who you are, where you're from and what you believe. Cows, for example, are readily

---

1 Just for the record, two weeks in Ibiza eating dodgy takeaways doesn't count as either intrepid travelling or adventurous dining. Silly maybe, but not adventurous.

2 If you cut two circles from a pair of really old leather shoes, roll them in sand, boil them hard, fry them and eat them with a spoonful of salt, then you are part way there to imagining how they taste. I'm not a fan.

3 This is working on the assumption that you accept it is more 'normal' (or at least 'less wrong') to eat some species over others.

eaten in the UK but are sacred in India. We love horses as pets, but the French also love them for lunch. Pork chops are savoured by Christians, but avoided by Muslims. Whereas I grew up seeing friends (and my little brother) keep guinea pigs as squeaky, noisy pets, I saw them barbecued on roadside stalls in Ecuador. My point is that people have a long-standing relationship with eating animals. While there is no doubt that, with an ever-increasing global human population, we need to drastically cut our consumption of meat. There are human health benefits, animal welfare benefits and environmental benefits to be gained from eating no, or at least less, meat. That's not me campaigning or trying to change your mind or anything. The world is an ever-changing place and in order to combat many of the problems on the horizon or, in many cases, scarily closer than we'd like to imagine, then we need to make changes now. This isn't just logic. It's science. Backed by research and supported by data. If you can see a big hole in the path ahead, do you keep walking and hope the fall won't hurt too much? Or do you change your path?[4] If we can respond sensibly as individuals, then it shouldn't be any different for us as a species, and looking ahead, there are some gaping holes in the path of humanity. Which route will we take, I wonder.

In terms of food, Africa is no different to any other place on the planet. It's a vast patchwork of different countries, different cultures and different menus. One thing that is however consistent across much of this wonderful red continent is the presence of bushmeat. It might be a term you've heard of and maybe you have a general idea about what bushmeat is. It's quite obviously meat, from the bush, right? Well, yes, it is, but that doesn't help us. What sort of meat? Which bush? We need a definition, which isn't as easy as you might anticipate, but

---

4 I'm assuming (and desperately hoping) you opted to sidestep the big hole, rather than stubbornly refuse to change where you walk and hope, as you plummet down, that there aren't too many sharpened spikes and crocodiles at the bottom.

probably no less than you'd expect after hearing this much about conservation by now. Some define it simply as wild-caught mammal species from African forests. Others define it as meat coming from non-domesticated species of birds, reptiles, amphibians *and* mammals from tropical forests around the world. Some people include various invertebrates, such as giant African land snails, within the definition. Although I'm keener on the broader definition, I'm unsure whether I would include snails, insects, spiders and their relatives.

One group that often appears in lists of bushmeat are the primates. There are differences between which species are eaten, and culturally, whether they're eaten or not, in fact. In Madagascar, for example, communities surrounding the breathtakingly biodiverse Andasibe-Mantadia National Park traditionally hunt various lemurs, but not the indri.[5] The indri is the largest of the lemurs and if I stopped being a scientist for a few seconds, I'd say that it looks like a big cuddly teddy bear with vivid green eyes and a panda-esque coat of contrasting black and white. They bound through their thickly forested habitat, leaping from tree trunk to tree trunk. They have one of the most distinctive calls within the animal kingdom. Sounding like a cross between a child's party trumpet and the world's largest, loudest creaking door, they can be heard from at least a kilometre away. And it is this, bizarrely, which for generations kept them safe from the bushmeat markets. Madagascar is a boiling pot of myriad beliefs and legends and it is bad luck (or 'fady') to break these traditions.[6] One of my favourite stories is

---

5 As so often happens with various species of animals and plants, their name (possibly) comes from a miscommunication between local guides and foreign explorers or early scientists. In Malagasy, 'indri' means 'Hey, look over there'. So, a well-meaning guide pointing out a weird animal to some white guy traipsing through the forest in the 1700s is forever immortalised.

6 Often with dire consequences for those committing the cultural faux pas, intentionally or otherwise.

that of a father and son who, long ago, went into the forest to collect honey. Something went wrong and the pair became separated. Having lost his son, the father called and called as he searched for him. He called for so long that the forest finally stepped in and, taking pity on the father, transformed him into the indri, so he could call for his lost child until the end of days. The Malagasy name for this enigmatic primate is 'babakoto', which means 'father of a little boy'. Communities there have always used this legend as a warning and avoid hunting indris, maybe out of respect, maybe out of fear. Unfortunately, this changed when political instability flared up in the early 2000s, and with the displacement and movement of communities around Madagascar, people who did not grow up with babakoto as part of their local belief system were more than happy to kill and eat them. I love this story, because it demonstrates not only the role of anthropology in conservation work, but also how much variation can be seen within neighbouring communities and the need to tailor conservation efforts accordingly. Despite this wonderful opportunity for grass-roots, deeply established conservation work based firmly in cultural beliefs, indris are critically endangered and although there may now be as few as 1,000 individuals left, this may drop by a further 80 per cent in the next thirty years, unless anything is done. Fingers crossed, hey!

Great apes feature heavily in the bushmeat trade wherever they're found, and chimpanzees are no exception. Although an estimated 500 species of animals feature within the African bushmeat trade, gorillas, bonobos and chimpanzees are particularly affected. Being large-bodied and arboreal[7] means they're easy to target (and shoot), and having extended childhoods and long periods between births, hunted populations take a long time to recover. Having distinctive life histories

---

7 Referring to the tree-dwelling critters, as opposed to those terrestrial ones stuck on the ground.

Tender loving care. Rhinoceros looks after her young baby, caring for her for years.

like this is often associated with intelligent social species, but can mean conservation disaster when these same animals are targeted by hunting or hit by habitat destruction.

When you visit a chimpanzee sanctuary, the differences are everywhere. Different countries. Different habitats. Different chimps. One thing they share however, is that almost every single chimp there has been affected by the bushmeat trade, and almost all are the indirect victims of hunting. You can't just walk into a forest and grab a baby chimp, it doesn't happen. You have to kill their mum, and probably others within the group, for their meat. Any babies are a bonus. They're hardly worth eating but they are worth tens of thousands of dollars in the pet trade. But that's why we see so many orphans – the tragic by-products of the bushmeat trade.

I could've chosen absolutely any of the kids I know to use as victims of the trade. Gola, Sweetpea, Max – all lost their mums to hunters' rifles. Billy, Jojo and Ella are orphans too. Portia, Jack, Sapo, Poppy and Chance. Even my beloved Pasa. The list goes on. But, for some reason, I'm drawn to one little guy over the others. At Jimmy and Jenny's place, the larger and older kids are housed in the Pavilion, which is a big holding area separated into a row of tall, solid cages, opening on to a metal-meshed arena. I'm not sure 'arena' is the right term but it's somewhere between a cage and a bizarre school playground. It's where the bigger chimps spend most of the day, although this will change when Jimmy and Jenny move to the mangrove forest and the proper sanctuary is set up. Every time I visit, it's a mad cacophony of noise – fighting, playing and psychological warfare, by the look of it.[8] I remember when I first arrived and was trying to learn names and faces, one little boy stood out. While the lovely Sweetpea is easy to recognise by her size, distinctive face and goofy smile, this fella was harder to recognise, for me at least, initially. As I scanned his face for the features I'd need to rely on to make an accurate ID, I noticed instead that Winner has three nipples. I burst out laughing when I registered this, but it meant I became exceedingly good at scanning and counting quickly in those early days.[9]

I've chosen Winner because he's probably my favourite boy within the group. He's sweet – something I'd rarely say about chimps – and he

---

8 All of which is reassuringly 'normal' for any happy group of chimps, captive or otherwise.

9 It's amazing which unexpected skills you develop as a biologist.

is one of life's true underdogs, which instantly makes him more interesting. He was found in an area called Zorzor, close to the border with Guinea. Jenny tells me that he was discovered by a westerner who was working in the area. Winner was locked in a tiny crate in the middle of the village. He'd been troublesome because 'he got into things' and as a result, was kept subdued in a prison so small he could hardly stand. He was let out once a week, when his new human friend visited, to make sure he had a taste of freedom. Other than these short reprieves, this orphan sat in the cage day and night, for over a year. It makes me feel sick to imagine him there and what would've happened when this 'troublesome' chimp became too big for the cage. I have no doubt he'd have been killed. Now, Winner lives with his new family, but the legacy of being locked away will never leave him. He finds it hard to mix with others and doesn't defend himself against them. He's

Leftovers. After his mother was shot for bushmeat, Winner was kept in a small cage for over a year.

Safe at last. Poppy, and every orphan, is a by-product of the bushmeat trade.

picked on and gets easily upset. Jenny has done all she can in terms of reshaping group dynamics for the kids, but the truth is that these animals have unimaginably traumatic starts to their lives and the experiences stay with them. Thankfully, there is every chance that Winner will settle down and eventually become more confident. Again, as with so many things, moving to the new forest home will make the world of difference to Winner, and all the orphan chimps in Liberia.

Winner's story is tragic, but if you think it's unique or even especially bad then you've got another think coming. Winner is yet another by-product of the horror of the bushmeat trade. One of countless orphans. One of innumerable victims. But surely the bushmeat trade is something we need to look at sensitively? It's an essential need… poor African people taking advantage of a necessary (and free) source of protein, right? This is where the problem of bushmeat grows to become a complicated and far-reaching one. Yes, bushmeat represents a much-needed source of protein for some of the world's poorest people and they're doing what their ancestors have done before them, using techniques and sometimes hunting trails that stretch back millennia. However, there is a different side to the problem when it also forms the basis of a lucrative international crime phenomenon. Bushmeat costs more to buy than chicken, goat or beef. It is often transported from rural forest areas to major African cities, where it is eaten as a delicacy, or goes on to be transported internationally. I can almost guarantee that African bushmeat has been illegally smuggled into a city close to where you're sitting now. Bushmeat is big business.

As with so many areas of conservation, bushmeat is one of those topics that could fill a whole book. It involves multiple people from multiple communities, at multiple socio-economic levels. It impacts multiple species in various habitats. It forms an impossibly complex commodity chain, starting (from a broad perspective) with rural hunters and ending with urban consumers. As a rule, hunting is opportunistic and much of the meat within the trade is smoked to preserve it, meaning it can be transported further afield. From the perspective of a biologist, the bushmeat trade has three major impacts. First, it drives biodiversity loss, clearing forests of much of the life that makes them so special. It increases the extinction rate (and likelihood) of individual species, either because they're targeted in particular or, as

Never try to catch a playful chimp. Jack evades capture during a game.

in the case of great apes, cannot recover from the impact of even moderate levels of hunting. Finally, commercial bushmeat hunting drastically escalates the hazard of 'new' zoonotic diseases (those that can be passed between human and non-human animals) being unleashed on the world. And here's where I'm going to swerve off what could be a jumble of thoughts about bushmeat in Africa. There are already lots of projects focused on dealing with it on a local and national scale. Good work is going on across Africa (as well as Madagascar), the neotropics and Asia, which focuses on providing people with alternative livelihoods and different sources of protein, as well as additional law enforcement and education, for everyone from school kids and community groups to teachers and even members of the judiciary. As a rule, this works very well. In some places, entire communities develop new skills in keeping livestock or rearing captive-bred animals such as cane rats, which they would otherwise take from the forest. This is great and definitely needs to continue, but while this work is on a local and national level, bushmeat on an international scale remains devastating to the wildlife affected and has the potential to be unimaginably dangerous for us too.

While writing this book, news has been released of discoveries made on a couple of occasions as I was covering that specific idea or topic, and the same is true now. I read an article this morning that instantly grabbed my attention. It has been shown, for the first time, which species of wildlife hosts the deadly Ebola virus.[10] Although it's long been suspected, this new research shows that the wild host is a bat, the greater long-fingered bat, in fact. While further research might show that other species also act as Ebola reservoirs, this important news means we might be better equipped to identify, monitor and ultimately

---

10 We call this a wildlife reservoir. The pathogen sits in the species, where it has very possibly co-evolved and co-existed alongside it for thousands or millions of years.

prevent deadly outbreaks. The second thing that grabbed my attention is that Jimmy is plastered all over the article. As well as being the co-founder of LCRP and responsible for the veterinary care of the chimps, he has been working hard leading a team of vets, epidemiologists and immunologists for a worldwide project under EcoHealth Alliance, studying the connections between human and wildlife health. Jimmy and his colleagues have shown for the first time that there is a discernible link between this terrible disease and wildlife. Ebola is just one of many zoonotic diseases that affects us in our modern world.

I've mentioned the problem with zoonotic disease (or zoonoses[11]) a few times and they are an issue, but the international trade in commercial bushmeat turns a middle-sized problem into a global, ticking time bomb. Have a quick think about some of the worst disease pandemics[12] throughout modern history and you'll soon see what the link is. The Black Death (or the Great Plague) arrived on fleas that hitched a ride on the back of black rats and throughout the medieval period killed between 30 and 60 per cent of the human population across Europe. Spanish flu, which broke out in 1918 and claimed the lives of up to an unbelievable hundred million people worldwide, originated from a virus found in pigs, we think. These historical horrors admittedly aren't all because of bushmeat, but they go to show how serious zoonoses are. More recently the global HIV outbreak evolved from something called SIV in non-human primates. In 2015, the World Health Organisation put together a list of the top emerging diseases which are 'likely to cause severe outbreaks in the near future'. It's a scary list in its own right, but what's really chilling is that all the

---

11 If you're wondering, it's pronounced 'zoo-no seez'.

12 A pandemic is like an epidemic but significantly scaled up. To qualify, a disease outbreak has to occur on a large scale, must be seen across international boundaries and must be infectious. In its most basic terms, it's a global outbreak.

diseases on this list are zoonotic and caused by what we call RNA viruses. This means the viruses are different to most 'typical' cells you might encounter. Rather than store their genetic material in the more familiar DNA, these viruses use RNA instead. A major difference is that RNA viruses have a limited genetic code, which means they can't fend off genetic mutations in the same way DNA can. The result is that they mutate, a lot. From the perspective of an Evolutionary Biologist, it's great because they can mutate and adapt to an ever-changing world. From the perspective of someone who doesn't want to be in the middle of the next global pandemic, it's bloody scary because it means they can change hosts, develop new ways of transmission, increase their impact, are harder to kill, and so on and so on. Newly emerging zoonoses pose a massive threat to our deeply interconnected modern global community. These animal viruses can mutate and take hold in us but if they happen to hook up with, for example, a flu virus, they can spread very rapidly indeed. Something like Ebola has a high mortality rate, up to 70 per cent in some outbreaks, but is (luckily) relatively hard to pass on between people. Imagine if it mutated with a flu virus and produced a new disease, which combined the deadliness of Ebola with the easy transmission of the flu. It might sound like the stuff of Hollywood disaster movies but if you combine high mortality with rapid and easy transmission, then it could be 'goodnight humanity' in no time. Imagine something so devastating starting from the blood of a bat on a small market stall somewhere, or from a piece of smoked monkey leg smuggled into France, the US or the UK.

It sounds as though I'm really trying to scare you, right? Look how quickly I've moved from talking about how cute Winner is to the end of humanity. We've seen already how diseases are able to jump between animals and humans with devastating impact. It's also pretty noticeable that some of the worst of these diseases, such as HIV, Marburg and Ebola, have potential links with the bushmeat trade. But what is the

Charred remains. Bushmeat isn't always a staple for 'poor African communities' and in many places is five times more expensive than pork or chicken.

chance that a piece of bat or rodent or primate meat ends up in a market near you? Tiny? Well, the bad news is that the answer reads like the last bit of this unholy trinity, because bushmeat is everywhere. In a report recorded across a four-year period, the U.S. Customs and Border Protection agency picked up over 69,000 pieces of bushmeat coming into the country. Although it sounds like a lot, this is likely to be massively below the real total. At JFK airport in New York in the US, bushmeat from green monkeys, mangabeys, baboons and chimpanzees has been detected. Testing has shown that some of this meat carried viruses capable of infecting humans.[13] The UK is no different and in 2012 an investigation found bushmeat for sale in various London markets. In 2014, DEFRA reported that in a single year, around 40 tonnes of meat was confiscated coming into the UK from across the world, although it doesn't specify how much of this was bushmeat. The

---

13 Despite having been smoked, which many people believe kills anything like bacteria or viruses within the meat.

Ella enjoys a mouthful of watermelon.

most detailed recent report (from 2010) comes from findings at Charles de Gaulle Airport in Paris, France. The contents are staggering: 2,500kg of bushmeat was discovered in one confiscation alone. It is estimated that, at the time of this study, 5.25 tonnes of bushmeat were coming through every week and, if the numbers are correct, then over 270 tonnes of illegal bushmeat flies in annually to this international airport. Unbelievable, hey. Why aren't we addressing it? Why aren't our governments being proactive and averting this pandemic cataclysm? The answer is, as ever, complicated. Because most of the transported bushmeat is smoked (which gives it a dried-out, charred and blackened appearance), it's hard to reliably identify the species, making it difficult for the average border official to distinguish something like chimpanzee meat from cow or goat, which are okay to transport. There is little or no existing data with which to formulate policy, and the truth is that it's just not seen as a priority. In an age where there are perceived to be more immediate, serious threats at our international borders, such as arms smuggling, human trafficking and the ever-present fear of terrorists and acts of terrorism, the 'what if' scenario of bushmeat and an as yet non-existent disease outbreak isn't near the top of anyone's worry list, it seems.

Of course, in my mind, the need to save our closest living relatives is justification enough to address the bushmeat trade, but we're a funny and sometimes selfish species, and maybe the danger that bushmeat poses to our own kind is what it'll take to make us step up for these iconic ape species.

Winner is now safe and will continue settling into a happy and secure life with the Desmonds but, until we take the commercial bushmeat trade seriously, chimpanzee sanctuaries and the work they do are still very much in demand.

# SAMANTHA'S STORY

A litany of
pain for a
research chimp

After years of research and
torture in a laboratory, Samantha
is once again in a forest habitat.

A few years back, when I did my PhD research, I found myself in the Caribbean. I had thought long and hard about the work I wanted to do for my doctorate and after innumerable mishaps, misadventures and misunderstandings[1] during my time in Africa and Asia, something deep within was definitely telling me to head to the Caribbean. Maybe it was because so little had been done to study the primates found across those islands, or maybe it was because, by looking at those green monkeys[2] taken from Africa to the Caribbean during the transatlantic trade in enslaved Africans, I would be able to really investigate those mysterious first steps associated with one species developing into another, new one. It had absolutely nothing to do with the fact that while there, I lived in a beautiful mountaintop house all on my own, or that there were miles and miles of chalk-white sand, or even that my nearest neighbours were wild monkeys and the only fight for space on the beaches was between the giant leatherback turtle mothers silently digging nests at night, so their delicate young could develop and hatch in peace. Nope, I hardly noticed how amazing this patch of paradise was. Honest.

I was based across three islands collecting genetic data and scans of skulls, to look for differences between the original African and introduced Caribbean populations, and at any possible differences between the three introduced Caribbean island groups. I was doing the Darwin's finches stuff from the Galapagos but with Caribbean monkeys instead.[3] Famously, these little birds across the islands of the Galapagos

---

1 If having half my project accidentally burned down, encountering overly inquisitive lions, corrupt local cops and an accident resulting in a broken back count as mishaps, misadventures and misunderstandings.

2 Most people know them as vervets but the classification for this group has been changed and is still up for some debate.

3 I called my thesis 'Primates of the Caribbean'.

Uneasy neighbours. Two adult green monkeys groom close to a biomedical facility in the Caribbean.

all have different sized and shaped beaks depending which island they live on and what food they eat, having adapted and evolved accordingly. Seed-cracking beaks are big and solid, insect-eaters have a slender beak and those which use tools (which is a very cool thing for a bird to do) are short and slightly curved. Because the introduced monkeys I studied are not native to the Caribbean and have no real predators or competition there, their populations exploded. When they started being a problem for the local wildlife, such as rare ground-nesting birds, and, after destroying whole fruit crops, became agricultural pests, the governments on these three islands introduced a culling policy.

Even as a conservationist, I believe the best thing is for them to be controlled in this way. My research involved firing lasers at freshly cleaned skulls obtained from recently shot animals. It wasn't especially nice work but, by doing this, I would be able to unlock more of the processes involved with the evolution of island species and, if my work showed that any of these monkeys were in fact part of the newly developed species or even subspecies, then I might have been able to help them in some small way by offering some level of conservation protection, even if the population did need to be reduced somewhat for the benefit of the other island-dwelling species. Rightly or wrongly, they are part of the ecosystem now and have been for many generations, for hundreds of years. On one of the islands where the monkeys are found, the way I collected my data was slightly different. I usually worked directly with the authorities and took samples from animals collected straight from the wild,[4] but things on the third island were different. If I wanted to work with samples on this island, then I would need to collect specimens myself, from a biomedical facility.[5] The monkeys were caught in the wild and people would receive a financial reward for delivering them to the research lab. Local people made extra cash, the authorities saw the pesky monkey population take a hit and the biomedical facility had a ready supply of fresh research 'participants'… everyone benefitted. Apart from the poor monkeys that ended up there, that is. The wild-caught green monkeys supplemented a breeding colony at the lab also. They were used for a whole range of testing but mainly to develop vaccines and screening tests for polio. A quick search online revealed that experimentation took place there but also that the monkeys (and their body parts) were shipped around the world. This facility had been running for almost forty years and reading that they had a blood bank made up from samples from 30,000 different animals gives a sense of the scale of the work that was done here, and in other facilities like it around the world.

I did not want to go. It was hard enough to justify my work with culled wild monkeys but this was at a whole different level. In my

---

4 I know many people will read this and think it was wrong or even question how I could have done it, seeing as I love my primates so much. The answer isn't a simple one but I did put a lot of thought into it. The culling was happening either way. In my mind, my work was turning what was undeniably a sad practice into something more constructive, with lots of potential benefits.

5 I won't name it but it wouldn't take much to discover where I am talking about, or which well-known island favoured by tourists housed this facility.

mind, my research just was not worth it. I believed that, by going along, I would be in some way supporting animal experimentation and vivisection. I'd have blood on my hands (both metaphorically and literally) and, being completely honest, I didn't want to see what went on there.[6] However, I decided to go. I did need to collect my data but it was more than that. I have always opposed animal experimentation and did my fair share of taking part in protests when I was at university. It's needless, vile and inhuman. It's even dangerous for humans, because of fundamental differences between us and even our closest primate relatives. Some experiments lead to serious consequences on occasions. Paracetamol, for example, is deadly to non-human primates but not us; some asthma drugs are harmless to primates but lethal to humans; and simple conditions, such as the common cold, can be deadly to chimpanzees and other primates, but obviously not to us, usually. With differences such as these, it's hard to justify the use of animals (let alone non-human primates) in such biomedical research. It was self-evident to me; a case of black and white, good against bad. I was firmly against the use of animals being tested. Humans weren't worth it. Who the hell do we think we are to torture another thinking, feeling, sentient being for our benefit? Then my mum fell ill.

I was at home for a weekend, and we were due to go shopping and have lunch. This was long before I started my PhD or ever stepped foot in a primate research lab. I had just started my undergraduate degree, but already felt passionately against the use of animals for biomedical research. We were getting ready to go out when Mum collapsed in front of me and was rushed to hospital. A blood clot had formed on her brain and had ruptured. Terrifying. Sitting in the ambulance with her, holding her hand,

---

6 I'm a big supporter of the idea that we should face our fears head-on. I'm scared of heights, so did a skydive and bungee jump. When I was younger, I was scared of death, so got a job in a funeral parlour. Even now, I'm still scared of clowns... but I'm not brave enough to head to a circus yet. Some things are too scary.

waiting as she spent hours in surgery. Watching in the months that followed to see how she'd recover; to see how much of my mum had been claimed by the brain haemorrhage and how much my dad, brother and I would get back. It was the worst period of my life and not one I would wish on anyone. But, oddly, it did give me time to think. About a whole range of things. I found myself exploring my views on death, the importance of family and the need to live in the 'here and now'. It also forced me into reassessing my own values. As I watched Mum lying there fighting, again and again my feelings seemed to conflict with my 'knowings'.

My concrete set of ideals needed to be much more nuanced than I had previously realised. I went from 'right and wrong' to 'sometimes, wrong can be right and other times, right might seem wrong'. Besides, what even is right or wrong, anyway? One of the things to come from this whole terrible episode is how subjective we can all be. I had always said that no human life was worth the experimentation carried out on primates and other animals, but here I was, grateful for every life taken and every experiment that went into saving my mum's life. In those horrible first moments and hours, I'd have given every chimpanzee. I'm not saying it was right, but equally, I'm not saying it was wrong. I know many will read this and judge me and that's fine. I wanted to draw in the idea that, even as someone who remains opposed to animal testing, situations change and we need to look at everything, whether it's science, history, economy, law or philosophy, both in a 'bigger picture' sense and in terms of how they affect those immediately around us, human and otherwise.

I walked into the Caribbean facility on my first day. I had to promise not to take photos, burn the place down, give it any bad press,[7] and so

---

7 Although my legal team might disagree, I still don't think I'm guilty of that here. I've not said which facility, haven't given any unfair coverage and haven't told you to boycott the area. I feel it's fair that we should all know what goes on and how the animals are sacrificed to save our lives.

on and so on. It's well hidden, in fact, by a cleverly placed monkey sanctuary, where smiling families visit to see the monkeys and other wildlife happily roaming around.[8] You'd be forgiven for never suspecting there was a major biomedical facility on the grounds, effectively hiding in plain sight. I'm not sure what I was preparing for – some Bond-villain dungeon scene, or maybe a sterile super laboratory, bright strip lights bleaching everything in a soulless white glow. It was far worse than either. It was nice. There was a nice garden, full of nice bright flowers and plump buzzing bees. Nice single-storey buildings were made from colourful bricks, windows opened invitingly. Friendly staff milled about and they were nice too. I was shown around the facility, to where the monkeys were housed. I expected to be deafened by screaming wild primates, desperate to escape. I imagined a scenario where I ran along rows of cages, releasing primate prisoners back to the wild before I was wrestled to the ground by burly security guards. Even now, I remember contemplating what it would be like in a Caribbean jail, before the British consulate (hopefully) stepped in. But it wasn't like that. I didn't mount an escape. Didn't end up in jail. Because I didn't see any screaming monkeys. I did see lots of monkeys, however. There were easily hundreds of them, maybe more. But they weren't screaming; they were nearly all united in silence. Row upon row upon row upon row of cages held adult monkeys. Most were housed on their own, in cages barely larger than them. Green monkeys are about the size of a big cat. They're not big but, like any animal, they need their space. There was enough room for them to stand up and enough room to turn around, but not much else. I remember walking through the section where the males seemed to be housed. Aggressive boys, who, in the wild, would happily tear each other's ears off if a neighbour even

---

8 Some of you cynical bunch might suggest this is a sneaky ploy to hide some rather gruesome practices behind something far more cute, cuddly and (importantly) acceptable.

looked at them in the wrong way. Here, in their cages, only thin mesh walls separated them. I crouched to look at one bruiser, careful not to get too close in case I stressed him out. He didn't care. Didn't scream. Didn't try to get away or even throw himself at the bars to get at my throat.[9] He didn't even flinch. His mahogany red eyes were sunken. They flickered listlessly towards me, hardly registering my presence, before he settled on the cage floor once again. I was disconcerted at how quiet it was, how the roof, made from that corrugated plastic sheeting which becomes brittle and breaks in the sun, was split in places allowing incongruous beams of shimmering light to dance across this desperately sad scene. I remember how hot it was. How it was so dry my mouth was parched in moments. I remember despairing at how mundane it seemed. That in this inviting compound sat countless prisoners, who had all but given up on life and who were unrecognisable compared to their loud, squabbling wild counterparts. One male bared his teeth and lunged at me. He upset me the most, because his spark was still burning. I assumed that, for him at least, it still hurt as much as I imagined it would.

*

Whether you support or oppose the use of animals in medical research that helps benefit humans, the consensus is that, in the future, we need to look for alternatives. Many people oppose animal testing. Animals do not make good comparisons for humans and there are countless moral reasons against using any animal, let alone our nearest living relatives, in these physically demanding and emotionally traumatic experiments. The numbers of animals used is decreasing, which is obviously great news. But lots of animals are still used in medical experimentation. Overall, around the world, approximately 58 million

---

9 I would have loved either of these responses. Both would have been natural behaviours for wild primates.

animals were used in 2017. The Home Office reports that, in the same year, an incredible 3,721,744 animals were used in the UK alone. These were mostly fish, mice, rabbits, rats, dogs and monkeys.[10] In 2007, the European parliament passed a legal recommendation that primates should be phased out of medical use across the European Union. Over ten years have now passed and regrettably there's still no ban. There are whispers that we might see it by 2025. Here's hoping.

The good news is that, almost everywhere, chimpanzees are no longer used in biomedical experimentation.[11] But this wasn't always the case and while there are (and always were) bigger threats to chimpanzees in the wild than medical testing, it is still something that has taken a toll, maybe more in terms of its impact on morality and human decency than on actual population numbers. Yet again, Liberia has an example for us. As is so often the case, it seems that this little coastal country can be used to highlight an aspect of chimpanzee conservation in a way that few others can. Sometimes there are clear reasons for doing something. Take the location of many historical biomedical laboratories that focus on primates, for example. A British or American pharmaceutical company or research group would, instead of basing the facility in the leafy countryside of England or the suburbs of an American city,[12] often set up shop on the other side of the world. Some argue that it is more humane not to transport the animals thousands of miles to a new country, or that it is done because the climate will be more appropriate for the animals and again, better for them.

---

10 In fact, 2,215 monkeys were used for testing in the UK. The total number across Europe is around four times higher than this, and then, in the US, 71,000 monkeys were used for biomedical research. Usually, monkeys are used in testing new drugs.

11 And that where they are, it is only when something as serious as 'in the interests of national security' can be used as a justification.

12 Although this did, and does, still happen in our own countries too, remember.

There are other reasons that, as I become older and more cynical, I tend to gravitate towards. It's cheaper not to have to move so many animals,[13] first of all. The other, darker reason is that the ethics in the countries where experimentation facilities are sometimes based are often far less rigorous than in the country where the company or institute is actually based, meaning they can legally get away with a lot more, for example, in Liberia than in America. The other reason is that, by tucking these facilities away on islands in the Caribbean or the Indian Ocean, or in a war-torn country in western Africa, far fewer people are there to raise the flag. 'Out of sight, out of mind' has been used to hide some of the darkest atrocities we bipedal apes have committed on both our own species and our non-human relatives. I could pick almost any example here but what happened in a small hidden mangrove in Liberia shows perfectly[14] how medical testing has affected both wild chimpanzees and our relationship with the species. This is the story of Samantha.

Samantha was born probably at some point during the summer of 1974. Not much is known about the first eighteen months or so of her life. It's safe to say she would have played with other members of her group. I'm fairly sure that, like any chimp, she would have been mischievous. I can say with certainty that she would have loved her mum and would have been loved in return. I am also 100 per cent certain that her mum was shot and that Samantha would have been plucked from her dead or dying body. My final certainty is that this innocent chimp had no idea of the torture that would lie ahead for the next four decades of her life. Here's where it gets complicated. This is

---

13 In terms of an 'Occam's razor' approach to the world, it's amazing how often the answer 'because it's cheaper' is behind what should be a nuanced and complex decision.

14 The word 'perfectly' really isn't the right one here but, in a way, maybe it is.

why I mentioned my experience in the Caribbean laboratory and why I touched on the idea that we as a species have benefitted so much from experiments carried out on primates and other animals. The New York Blood Center (the NYBC) is a non-profit organisation, set up, it can't be denied, to improve the lives of millions of people. They provide products and services to around two hundred hospitals in the US and carry out research to make sure that this is done in an effective and safe manner. One area of research is to make sure that people who benefit from life-saving blood transfusions aren't accidentally given life-ending diseases at the same time. One such disease is hepatitis B. It affects the liver and is passed on through blood and other bodily fluids. It's a particularly nasty virus. The NYBC set about developing vaccines for a few different things, such as river blindness, but hep B was their main focus. To give patients the chance of a healthy life while screening blood for this virus[15] was an incredibly important undertaking. To achieve this admirable feat, the NYBC set up Vilab II in 1974, in Liberia.

Initially, young and wild chimpanzees were captured and taken to the facility where they were subjected to tests, biopsies[16] and other experiments. It's hard to know exactly what happened next because a lot of the records were later burned.[17] At some point, the decision was made to develop a breeding colony. Some people say this happened because so many young apes ended up accidentally hanging themselves after being

---

15 As someone who has worked with primates for a long time, has been scratched, and has been through the scary wait to see whether you've been infected with something such as hepatitis, I can say first hand that vaccines and treatments to remove this worry and reduce the threat can only ever be a good thing.

16 Where a small piece of the body is removed and tested for the presence or absence of a particular disease or infection. This can be done through using a hollow syringe-like piece of equipment or with a scalpel.

17 It will make more sense as the story progresses. Either way, it was still a cowardly act.

tethered to climbing frames by straps around their necks. Whatever the reason, the facility started a breeding programme. This is where Samantha comes into the story. I have managed to acquire a copy of her medical records from her time at Vilab II. The front of the file is a simple beige folder, with a brown tab in the top left-hand corner. On it is written #125 SAMANTHA ♀ on a dirty white label. The edges of the folder are tattered and worn but there's nothing special about the file. Nothing ominous. Inside, however, are seventy-nine pages. Some are tables filled with handwritten notes, some dental charts, and some are detailed lists. It is a catalogue of abuse. Over the next forty years or so, this innocent-looking folder details it all. The admission sheet records that she arrived at the facility on 14 December 1976, when she was estimated to be around eighteen months old. She wasn't weighed, teeth weren't checked, history unknown. The only other information is that she was 'DONATED BY MAN FROM SMELL NO TASTE'.[18] It's hard to sift through the various sheets. The anonymous handwriting varies, making it difficult to read, and is made trickier by the various shades of ink and levels of damage from the effects of both damp and sunlight. The veterinary jargon is heavy in places and some pages are simply filled with endless drug names and doses given. But going through Samantha's file tells a harrowing story. Between 1976 and 2007, Samantha was used for HIV, hepatitis B and hepatitis C testing. Blood 'cleaning' products were also used on her. She was anaesthetised 345 times. For anyone who has been under a general anaesthetic even once, the uncertainty, confusion and grogginess is all quite horrible. But we

---

18 And there it is. The only funny* bit in this chapter. There are indeed some rather obscure and random place names in Liberia.

* And while we're here, even this isn't funny really. It was given the name after American soldiers were stationed there during the Second World War. Sadly, local people could smell the good food being cooked in the soldiers' compound but could never taste it.

## VILAB II Animal History Sheet

I.D.#: 125   NAME: Samantha

| DATE '89 | WT (kg) | T° | P | R | PROTOCAL # | PROCEDURE USED | BIOP. | Hct | WBC | L | N | M | E | B | CLINICAL PROCEDURES Hx – Dx –Tx – Vacc. – TB Test. |
|---|---|---|---|---|---|---|---|---|---|---|---|---|---|---|---|
| 3/9–3/11 | | | | | | | | | | | | | | | Mebendazole 200mg S.I.D x3days |
| 4/4–4/6 | | | | | | | | | | | | | | | Mebendazole 200mg S.I.D x3days |
| 3/9–5/11 | | | | | | | | | | | | | | | Mebendazole 200mg S.I.D. x3 days |
| 5/19/89 | | | | | | Gave birth to ♀ child | | | | | | | | | observed the whole day... |
| 6/1/89 | 47.27 | | | | | | X | 44 | 8910 | | | | | | used serum for Alts–88 |
| 6/8–6/10 | | | | | | | | | | | | | | | Mebendazole 200mg S.I.D. x 5 days |
| 6/28/89 | 46.93 | 98.9 | 124 | 32 | | | X | 45 | 7040 | | | | | | Ket. 5ml t dose, TB test (Cooper's) |
| 2/17–2/19 | | | | | | | | | | | | | | | Mebendazole 200mg S.I.D. x3 days |
| 2/20/89 | 49.30 | 98.4 | 120 | 30 | | | X | | | | | | | | Ket. 6ml t dose |
| 11/14–11/16 | | | | | | | | | | | | | | | Mebendazole 200mg S.I.D. x3days |
| 12/12/89 | 37.27 | | 112 | 28 | | | X | | | | | | | | Ket. 6ml t dose, TB test (Cooper's) |
| 3/26–3/28 | | | | | | | | | | | | | | | Mebendazole 200mg S.I.D x3days |
| 3/9/89 | | | | | | | | | | | | | | | |

Samantha's file.

know what it's for. Imagine never knowing when the dart gun was coming. Not understanding what was happening. Imagine the fear she must have experienced. Never knowing whether one of the humans was bringing food or the painful sting of a dart. Forty-nine liver biopsies were performed on her. While under anaesthetic, an incision is made in her abdomen and a needle inserted between the ribs into the liver. A small piece of the organ is removed, so that it can later be examined under a microscope. There is also evidence from the reports of what seems like countless blood draws. Each time, the blood would have been used to see how Samantha was affected by an experiment or how a disease or infection was progressing. She was tested for TB again and again. Here she would have been restrained, then a small droplet of TB injected on to her eyelid. If you're wondering why the eyelid, it's because the soft tissue there is so sensitive, it shows any reaction with great clarity. It's also perfectly placed, as it is easy to see any reaction after the animal is awake without the need to get too close. A good example of something that might be 'perfect' for the humans involved but is far from ideal for those animals on the receiving end.

Reading through the file becomes increasingly distressing and I actually want to stop. I don't want to decipher the scrawled handwriting only to reveal more heartbreaking secrets. But I owe it to Samantha and feel she stands for something more now. She represents every great ape, monkey, dog, pig, rat, mouse and rabbit who didn't have a name. So I read on.

In 1980, Samantha would have been six years old. An age where wild chimpanzees start to celebrate their independence and begin exploring the world around them. It's also around the age when their bodies are maturing and so to reduce the threat Samantha may have posed to researchers, they simply removed her teeth one day. A few years later, in 1989, Samantha would have been a young adult and on 19 May, something wonderful happened: she 'gave birth to a female child'. But the child died within a day or so. There was no record of the name. On 20 November a year later, she gave birth again, this time to a baby boy. She was tranquillised to remove the baby that same day. He died also. Finally, in 1993, she gave birth to another daughter. She died. Both underweight and having never been taught by her own mother how to care for a baby, Samantha had little chance of success as a mum. Adding in the risk of infection posed by the conditions around her, there was even less hope. I'm not here to tug on the heartstrings or take advantage of the suffering of this non-human being but the thought of her there, confused and scared and then upset by the physical loss of her children, is something we should not brush over lightly. Whether they were removed by the team or as a result of their deaths, Samantha never got to bond with her children. Never got to nurse them, tickle them or guide them. It makes my chest heavy writing this but still, for their benefit at least, I'm glad they didn't make it. I think that, as a species, humans need to reflect on our responsibilities and that, sometimes, we need to hang our heads.

Then, in 2007, the American government decided to retire chimpanzees across the vast majority of the facilities where they had been used previously. Good news. The time of countless experiments and painful tests was over for the Liberian blood chimps at Vilab II. Samantha was safe. As a parting gift, the NYBC director promised 'lifetime care' for the chimps. The eighty-five remaining chimpanzees were rehomed across six islands in a tidal estuary, an area of slow-flowing salt water and beautiful mangrove habitat. Each island had a drinking station where the chimps could access fresh water and they were brought food daily by staff who used to work within the research facility, as the islands weren't big enough to provide food and the water was salty and not safe for drinking. This is a story of redemption for many of these people and I have seen how they deeply love the ex-research island chimps and the new orphans coming in. Samantha and the other chimps were free but still relied on humans to survive.

In fairness, the NYBC kept their promise for a few years but in 2015 they walked away, pulled funding and left the chimps to fend for themselves. They cited problems in working with the Liberian government and while I'm always happy to call out corruption and foul play when I see it, the government was not to blame. In my mind, it's 'out of sight, out of mind' again and I can only imagine the appeal of saving hundreds of thousands of dollars a year by not funding a bunch of chimps no one cared about. When asked, an NYBC spokeswoman said they 'never had any obligation to care for the chimps, contractual or otherwise'. They also said their support was 'entirely voluntary' and that it was offered on a 'philanthropic basis until the government of Liberia could take over'. Make of that what you will, but I don't think the most responsible time to leave was during the worst Ebola epidemic in the region,[19] after the country was still recovering from the devastating impacts of a brutal civil war. Any country would have struggled, let alone the fourth poorest on the planet. But maybe these things are above the understanding of a simple scientist and they had good reasons for abandoning the chimps with no food or water and blaming people who could barely afford to feed themselves, let alone these animals.

The drinking stations broke and there was no money for food. Those local people who just a few years before were laboratory staff were keeping Samantha and the others alive, paying for food from their own pockets and delivering cups of water to the desperate chimps via boats. Things were dire and the chimps were running out of time. Fortunately for them, this is when Jimmy and Jenny arrived, in 2015. Jimmy noted that in the ten years or so since being retired, the chimps had received no veterinary care and that lots of new babies had been born into the already fraught situation. Of the eighty-five chimps retired in 2007, Jimmy and Jenny arrived to find only sixty-six animals across the six islands. Having lost nineteen was bad enough but when you understand that, actually, this sixty-six includes twenty-one that were too young to have been from those originally retired, you realise that only forty-five of the eighty-five retirees survived. What happened to those animals we will never know, but while it's nice to think they died after living more natural lives on the islands, it is more realistic to say that starvation, dehydration and the effects of infections on their already weakened immune systems would more than likely have taken their toll instead.

When the Desmonds arrived, they sent me photos of the island chimps. Skeletally thin and screaming in fear, these were the most pitiful chimpanzees I have ever seen. Among them was an especially

---

19 Which killed around 11,000 people.

Walking dead. When the Desmonds arrived in Liberia, Samantha, Bullet and the other ex-research chimps were so thin, they were close to death.

gaunt and forlorn individual – and this was the first time I heard about the enigmatic Samantha. Having survived years of experimentation and subsequent abandonment, she had somehow clung on to life, but even from thousands of miles away, I could see she did not have long left. Then, with their indomitable spirit and seemingly limitless energy, the Desmonds did what they do best. They saved lives that needed saving. They mobilised better feeding regimes and ensured the chimps had water. They introduced contraceptive pills to make sure no more babies were born into a situation that could not cope with them, and finally, Jimmy was able to offer some much-needed veterinary care. Within the space of a few months, an almost unbelievable transformation had taken place. Jenny sent me more photos, of chimps who weren't screaming for scraps of food, but who looked relaxed and calm. Those same emaciated wretches had filled out with muscle once again and the

Looking ahead. Thankfully, Lucy will never know the type of traumas Samantha faced but, like every chimp in every sanctuary, has had a bad start in life. Her future however, is looking bright now that she's safe.

almost hairless apes were now replaced by animals showing beautifully glossy, healthy black coats.

Samantha is still on her island home. She is as healthy as can be expected and, considering what she has been through, she is as close to living a wild life as she is ever likely to. A big legal case followed and finally, the NYBC paid several million dollars. A well-known animal welfare charity is now responsible for Samantha and the others.[20] Jimmy and Jenny left this project but work close by, with the flood of orphans coming in.

I'm not going to say it's a happy ending because it's not. It's an okay ending at best. It's a truly awful story and while animal-based experimentation and research may not have had a hugely devastating impact on wild chimpanzee populations, it is nevertheless a part of the story that links our two species. It is a story that needs to be told. Samantha, and countless other chimpanzees like her, have been put through unimaginable stress, trauma and pain, and regardless of your views on this type of research, we all owe these incredible beings a huge debt of thanks. Thank you, Samantha. Thank you for saving the lives of so many people you will never meet. Thank you for never giving up. Thank you for showing us what true dignity looks like.

Knowing me, knowing you. I fail to see how anyone could look into the intelligent and emotionally-charged eyes of our nearest relatives like Lucy here and not see someone gazing back.

---

20 But that's a story for another time.

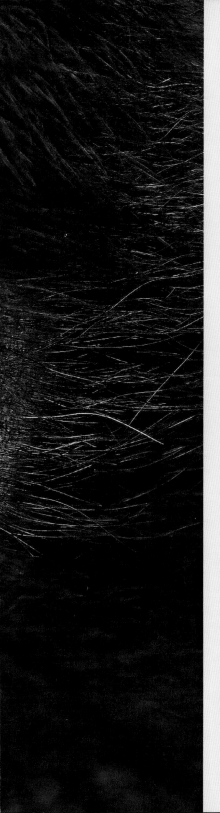

# THE REAL TARZAN'S JANE

Asking Dr Jane Goodall what the future holds for chimpanzees

I might as well tell you – I haven't always been an award-winning TV broadcasting, book-writing, mature and respectable evolutionary biologist.[1] I've had lots of different jobs, which, although I may not have entirely enjoyed at the time, I have learned from. I'm at the point in my career now where I am often asked by students how I got here, with the obvious hope that I'm about to give away the secret that will allow them to follow in my (very fortunate) footsteps. My answer is this: 'There is no right way, I got my lucky break serving soup.' It comes as quite a surprise to people when I tell them that I ended up working in chimpanzee conservation in Africa after being Jane Goodall's waiter one evening.

I had several jobs while at university, as I needed enough to eat, drink and buy the occasional book. For my first degree, I studied in Cambridge but not *at* Cambridge.[2] I did, however, work at Cambridge University, as a silver service waiter. For anyone who knows me even a little, this may not seem like an obvious fit for me, but I enjoyed my time there. In my third year I slipped and broke my wrist while walking my dog one icy morning and couldn't work for several months. On my first night back, though, I was waiting at a charity dinner and the guest of honour was Dr Jane Goodall. It's no exaggeration to say that, growing up, Jane was my hero. We have slightly different recollections of how the evening played out. In my mind, between each course, I deftly managed to drop in snippets of conversation over serving spoons and platters, perfectly demonstrating my confidence and readiness to work. Jane appears to remember some guy 'hovering', 'lurking' even, who managed to give her his entire life story in thirty-second chunks during dinner. Now is not the time to argue over exactly who is right

---

1 Believe it or not.

2 There are two very good universities in the city, one is just slightly more famous than the other.

(partly because I know I'd probably lose), but whichever way it came about, she finally told me to pull up a chair after I'd served the mints with the tea and coffee and we chatted briefly. A few weeks later I was in Uganda.

Jane led the way not just for those people wanting to study chimpanzees but, in many ways, for anyone who wanted to work with wild animals. She had travelled to Tanzania back in 1960, after making a connection with the renowned anthropologist Dr Louis Leakey. She was determined to work with African apes in the wild and despite not having a degree, she set about achieving her dream. At a time like this, it was considered improper for a young lady to head off to Africa on her own, so she'd needed to take someone to help make sure she was safe. She took her wonderful mum. Without being able to rely on the experiences of others, as nothing quite like what she was undertaking had been successfully done before, Jane had to work by trial and error, eventually managing to habituate the group of wild chimpanzees in a heavily forested area known as Gombe. After developing and managing one of the world's longest-running and best-known field sites for years, Jane became one of the foremost and most dedicated conservationists ever. Now, she travels for around 300 days a year, to places near and far, spreading her message of peace and gathering support from schoolchildren, industry leaders, rock stars and political figures to help make the world a better place. I still know Jane very well and from serving her soup to working for her in the forests of Uganda, I now sit on her charity board. Throughout it all, Jane has continued to work tirelessly for chimps and humans alike. I decided that I needed to ask her a few questions about why chimps are so important, what led her to where she is today and what the future might hold for our nearest living relatives. I mean, who better to ask than the person who knows chimpanzees the best?

**Ben:** *You have been working with chimpanzees since the 1960s, but I know your love of nature started when you were much younger. When and how did it all start?*

**Jane:** I was born loving animals. My first real experience in observation of animal behaviour was when I was four and a half years old. We lived in London and so I was very excited when my mother took me to stay on a farm and I saw cows, pigs, sheep and horses – all grazing or rooting in the fields. I was given the job of collecting the hens' eggs. They laid them in nest boxes around the small houses where they slept at night. Apparently, I began asking where the egg came out but got no satisfactory answer. I remember seeing a hen – she was brown – entering one of the hen houses. I must have thought that she was going to lay an egg – and decided I would watch for myself, so I crawled in after her. Big mistake – she flew out with loud squawks. I should have realised that no hen would go into that place – it was clearly dangerous with an inquisitive toddler in there. So I hid in another one and waited and waited. I was gone for four hours. My mother had been searching – everyone was worried. Yet when she saw her little girl running to the house, she saw the excitement in my eyes and instead of scolding me, she sat down to hear the wonderful story of how a hen lays an egg. I can still see that event so clearly. I love that story because it illustrates how lucky I was to have a supportive mother. My behaviour suggested the making of a scientist – the curiosity, asking questions, not getting the right answer and deciding to find out for myself, making a mistake, not giving up and learning the importance of patience. A different mother might have crushed that early scientific curiosity.

As I grew older, I spent hours outside, watching birds and squirrels and insects.

And I was ten when, after reading as many books on animals as I could (there was no TV back then!), I found the book *Tarzan of the Apes* and decided I would grow up, go to Africa, live with wild animals and write books about them.

For a girl to do something like that was unthinkable then. Also, we had very little money. Everyone told me to dream about something I could actually achieve – except my mother. 'If you really want to do that, you will have to work very hard and take advantage of all opportunities. But don't give up.' That is the message I take around the world today, especially in disadvantaged communities. And I wish Mum was alive to know how many people have said 'Thank you, Jane. You taught me that because you did it, I can do it too.'

**Ben:** *I know George Schaller had limited success working with mountain gorillas in the Virunga Mountains in the late 1950s but no one else had ever really followed wild apes for scientific research purposes, and much of what we knew about them was clearly wrong. What was it like being one of the very first people to successfully habituate and work with wild apes?*

**Jane:** I had watched and written about the creatures around my home as a child. I did not think about being one of the first in the field. I had no model to follow – did not know about Schaller's work when I began. Remember, I had not been to college and knew nothing about science or scientific methodology. I just followed my instincts. My job was to gain the trust of the chimpanzees, identify them as individuals, and gradually I knew I would learn about their behaviour.

**Ben:** *What were the main challenges you faced in working with wild chimpanzees in Tanzania in the 1960s and 1970s?*

**Jane:** My first challenge was that they were so shy. It took months to habituate them and it was thanks to David Greybeard, the one who lost his fear first, that gradually the others came to realise I was not a threat, after all. I was also worried about money – my little grant was for six months only. Fortunately, during the fourth month, I observed David Greybeard inserting grass stems into termite mounds, then picking off the soldier termites (with the big heads) and crunching them up in his mouth. Moreover, he picked leafy twigs, and, to use them as tools, had to strip their leaves. Only humans were supposed to be able to use and make tools as far as we knew at that time. It was because of that observation that the *National Geographic* became interested and agreed to provide funding for me to continue the study. And then sent photographer and film-maker Hugo van Lawick to record the study. Prior to the release of his films and photographs, some scientists had dismissed my observations – after all, I had not been to college. And I was a girl!

**Ben:** *What were the main findings of your work?*

**Jane:** Gradually, I learned about the very distinct personalities of the different chimpanzees. Over the years, we have found that there are good and bad mothers, and the offspring of the good mothers, who are protective but not over-protective, affectionate, playful and, above all, supportive, do better. These male offspring tend to rise higher in the hierarchy and are likely to sire more offspring, and the females make better mothers. We now know that different chimpanzee populations have different cultural behaviours, passed from one generation to the next as infants watch, imitate and practise particular behaviours such as tool use. Their postures and gestures of communication are much the same as ours and are often used in the same context – kissing, embracing, patting in reassurance, begging for food with a palm-up outstretched hand, are all so familiar to us. They are also capable of extreme violence. The males regularly patrol the boundaries of an established territory, and may brutally attack members of neighbouring communities, including older females. Only adolescent females, who have not given birth, are safe from attack by neighbouring males. At Gombe, we witnessed what can only be described as a primitive sort of war, when males of a larger community annihilated all members of a smaller community with the exception of the young females. Young females may transfer permanently into new communities, which minimises the risk of inbreeding. Others, after becoming pregnant, return to their home communities where they typically remain for the rest of their lives.

Chimpanzees are capable of compassion and true altruism, which is maybe best shown when an unrelated adult was seen to adopt an infant whose mother had died.

Because they are so like us, biologically and behaviourally, it enables us to understand those ways in which we are most different. We have, for example, developed spoken language, enabling us to tell our children about things and events in an abstract way, make plans for the future, discuss ways of solving problems and so much more. It is traits such as these, I believe, which were a major driving force behind the explosive development of the human intellect.

*Ben: We have both been incredibly privileged to see wild chimpanzees do things that the majority of people will never experience. My favourite piece of chimp behaviour is watching two young chimps together, where one grabs the foot of their passing friend, eliciting hoarse giggles and an inevitable play-fight. It makes my heart soar every time I am lucky enough to see it. I know you have seen innumerable incredible things done by chimps, many of which have changed not only how we look at chimps, but, in many ways, at animals in a wider context. But is there one 'little' piece of chimp behaviour that you hold close to your heart?*

**Jane:** Oh Ben, I have spent so many, many, many hours (and hours and hours) with the chimps and have so many, many, many magical memories, but a few do stand out. In one, an adult female, Madam B, was fishing for termites. Her two-and-a-half-year-old daughter, Little Bee, was watching intently. When her mother moved to a new hole, Little Bee at once went to the place where her mother had been working. She picked up a *tiny* tool – at most it was 3 or 4 centimetres long, whereas normal termite fishing tools are, on average, nearer 25 centimetres in length. Well, Little Bee industriously poked her inappropriate tool into the hole that had yielded such good, crunchy food for her mother. Her attempts were futile, but she did not give up. And after about five minutes… wow! One of the delicious soldier termites, those with the big red heads, was clinging to the end of her minute tool. Little Bee stared in amazement. For a moment, she was motionless – then she pulled off the termite with her teeth and with a grimace, she threw the tool away and chomped repeatedly on the prize, still grimacing. Continuing to chew, she climbed a tree above the termite mound. What was she thinking?

**Ben:** *Why did you want to work with chimpanzees? What's the appeal?*

**Jane:** I would have studied ANY animal – I was fortunate enough that Louis Leakey suggested the most fascinating – and the longer I studied them, the more I learned, and the more fascinated I became. The study, carried on by students at the Gombe Stream Research Centre, is now approaching its sixtieth year of unbroken observation.

**Ben:** *You have had so many successes as an academic. You developed and ran the Gombe Stream Research Centre, the most renowned primate field-site in the world, and are responsible for nurturing the careers of many of the world's most successful primatologists, but you left research for conservation. Why did you make this switch in careers?*

**Jane:** In 1986, I went to a conference of scientists studying chimpanzees in a variety of places throughout their range. The aim was to find out how their behaviour differed depending on the different environments. Was there evidence of *cultural* behaviour (another word not accepted by mainstream science back then, but about which I had already written). We had a session on conservation, and I was shocked to see what was happening everywhere – chimpanzee numbers were dropping, this was the start of the commercial bushmeat trade: wire snares, shooting mothers to sell their infants, the destruction of the forests. And there was a session on conditions in some captive situations: the cruel training of chimps for the circus or other forms of entertainment; the horrendous treatment of chimps in medical research labs. I went to the conference as a scientist with the best life I could ever have wished for, but I left as an activist. I knew I had to try to do something to help.

**Ben:** *We all know that chimps are facing threats from a range of places and they're in trouble for multiple reasons. Is it the case that they are in greater danger than other species, or is it just that we have a greater awareness of their plight?*

**Jane:** Chimps, gorillas, orangutans and bonobos, as well as gibbons and many other primate species, are in trouble, along with elephants, rhinos, lions, giraffes and one of the most endangered, the pangolin. And so many other species, including species of plants, are threatened with extinction. In fact, we are in the middle of the sixth great extinction, which is being caused by human activities. One of the biggest concerns is the speed with which insect numbers are declining – without insects, many ecosystems will collapse, as without them acting as pollinators, our food crops will die. We need to make major changes in the way we exploit the natural world if we care about future generations.

**Ben:** *Does the use of chimpanzees as flagship ambassador species help the wider ecology in sub-Saharan Africa, or does it detract from the importance of each species and habitat, all of which need help?*

**Jane:** To save chimpanzees, we must save their forest habitats. And this, in turn, will save the biodiversity of those habitats. In this way, chimpanzees and other flagship species such as bonobos, gorillas, orangutans, elephants and rhinos all help to save countless other, less iconic, but nevertheless important, animals and plants.

**Ben:** *With fragmented populations affecting the genetic health of populations in general, rampant habitat destruction and a renewed thirst for the international bushmeat market and pet trade, do you think wild chimpanzees still have a chance?*

**Jane:** In the areas where the Jane Goodall Institute, and other conservation groups working in chimpanzee habitat, operates, the chimpanzees have a chance of surviving – but only if we align ourselves closely with local communities, alleviating poverty and helping people find ways of making a living that do not involve destroying the environment, such as cutting down trees to make charcoal. Because of JGI's holistic programme to improve the lives of the people living in and around chimpanzee habitat, local communities have become essential partners. They understand that protecting the environment is not just for the future well-being of the wildlife, but also for that of their own children.

**Ben:** *Can humans and chimpanzees successfully coexist in this modern world, or will we always be in conflict with one another?*

**Jane:** If local communities and, in some cases, corporations continue to penetrate ever deeper into chimpanzee forest habitats, either because of population growth, or business interests such as logging and mining, there will always be conflict unless we find innovative solutions. Protecting their forests and linking them with corridors is the best solution. And this will only happen if the local communities understand the importance of protecting the forest and that this can benefit them as well as the chimpanzees. Eco-tourism, for example, is a good means by which both can benefit, helping the chimpanzees and providing jobs and income to local communities. The communities around Gombe and other forests where JGI is working have become our partners in conservation in this way. None of this is easy but we must fight on. And we must confront human population growth worldwide. Only by working across all these levels together can we hope that chimpanzees and other forest wildlife will survive into the future.

**Ben:** *It is sometimes hard to remain optimistic when talking about conservation. How do you maintain your optimism?*

**Jane:** I have several reasons for hope. The first is the young people out there. Once they know the problems, once we listen to their voices, once we empower them to take action, nothing can stop them. Today there are so many strong, determined and courageous young people. I meet them everywhere. They are changing the world for the better. I also find our own brains quite amazing. We are constantly coming up with innovative technologies that will allow us to live in greater harmony with the natural world. And ways in which we can live our lives respecting the natural world. Nature itself is amazingly resilient and keeps me hopeful. The fact that there are no longer bare hills around Gombe, but instead the forest has returned. Little seeds can survive in the ground for long periods of time and, given a chance, they will restore nature where we have destroyed it, and animals can be rescued from the brink of extinction. I see social media as a reason for hope too. For the first time in human history, we can reach out to people globally and encourage them to show solidarity for a single cause. Before this, small groups who cared about something such as plastic pollution might feel isolated, whereas today they know their concern is shared around the world. This gives people and movements more strength. Finally, the indomitable human spirit keeps me full of hope. I meet or hear of so many people who tackle problems that seem impossible to solve. They persevere. Others join them because of their enthusiasm, and eventually they succeed. Nelson Mandela was released after twenty-three years in prison with the amazing ability to forgive and, with de Klerk, was able to bring the evil regime of officially sanctioned apartheid to an end in South Africa. Winston Churchill took on the task of defeating Nazi Germany. Martin Luther King led the fight against discrimination of African Americans. I have met many people with physical disabilities who refuse to allow this to depress them, and lead lives that are inspirational to those around them. My friend Gary Haun went blind when he was twenty-one. He decided to become a magician, which might seem impossible! Yet he persevered and does such wonderful shows for children that often, they do not even realise he is blind. Then he tells them that if things go wrong in their lives, they must never give up as there is always a way forward. He does scuba diving, skydiving and has even taught himself to paint.

**Ben:** *You inspire so many people around the world. I've seen you talk many times now and, on each occasion, I can see the impact you have on those in your audiences. But who or what inspires you to keep fighting?*

**Jane:** I am very obstinate, which helps me to keep fighting. My love of wild places constantly inspires me, and the energy and optimism I see in the children I spend time with always helps keep me going.

**Ben:** *There have been some dire warnings over climate change and species extinctions. What do we need to do at a society level to avoid such a bleak future?*

**Jane:** We need to address the issues of explosive (human) population growth around the world, alleviate poverty, and where possible, make changes in our lifestyle, to minimise our impact on the world we live in.

**Ben:** *What do we need to do as individuals?*

**Jane:** We each need to realise that every single one of us can make a difference. Although it may sound a simple task, it has the potential for having a huge impact. We each need to make the commitment to ethical choices such as not eating meat. Setting up or joining a Roots & Shoots[3] group is also a good way to get involved and make a difference.

**Ben:** *You must have met so many chimpanzees over the years. Do you have a favourite and why?*

**Jane:** Old David Greybeard and Flo will always hold a very special place in my heart.

**Ben:** *What would it mean if we did lose chimpanzees?*

**Jane:** The chimpanzees have been described as 'gardeners of the forest'. They swallow the seeds of the fruits they eat and spread them over a wide area in their poop. The loss of any species can have a ripple effect and lead to the collapse of the whole ecosystem. As they are our closest relatives, long-term studies of the different individual chimpanzee communities can help us better understand some aspects of our own behaviour. As there is still so much to learn about these long-lived, intelligent and emotional beings, it would be a tragedy for science if they were to disappear. But for me, the most important consequence of losing chimpanzees would be how future generations would judge us. How can we sit back and allow chimpanzees – and so many other species – to vanish during our watch? They have as much right to live as we do – each

and every one of them. We have stolen so much of their forest home, we have killed so many individuals, orphaned so many infants, caused so much suffering. Now we must fight to save them.

---

3 The Roots & Shoots initiative is central to how Jane (and the Jane Goodall Institute) works. Groups of young people, from playschool to university students all around the world, set up programmes where they work to make a positive mark on the world. Each project is unique and the only thing that links them (apart from Jane) is that each one focuses on people, species *and* the environment.

**Ben:** *What do you think the future holds for our nearest living relatives?*

**Jane:** It looks very bleak if we carry on as usual. This is why I travel constantly, everywhere, trying to wake people up. We must each do our bit, spread awareness, perhaps lobby, donate to those protecting the forests where the apes live, reduce our own carbon footprint to mitigate climate change, try to avoid buying products containing palm oil unless from truly sustainable plantations, lobby for labelling so consumers know what they are buying and so on. There is an endless list of ways everyone can help, and different people can make an impact in different ways. Corporations and businesses and governments can make the real change. But we make choices regarding which politicians are elected, and as consumers, we can influence businesses. What people do not buy, they will not try to sell. Only if we reduce poverty, change unsustainable lifestyles and confront human population growth can we expect a better world in the future, not only for our nearest living relatives but for humans. We depend on forests and the natural world for our own future. So let's all get together, and each of us do what we can. Then the future for the apes will be assured.

# SO WHAT CAN BE DONE?

## How can we really help chimpanzees?

Grub up. The orphans gather to drink tasty
formula, sometimes sharing with each other
but most often greedily slurping.

If you ask ten different people what they think it's like to work in conservation,[1] you'll probably get ten different answers. A lot of people seem to have the idea that conservation is about cuddling cute orphan animals and that you spend your days playing with baby tigers, pandas and orangutans. If you're thinking that, especially after getting this far into this book, then step away now. Conservation is not for you.[2] Others might come up with a few interesting answers or ideas but you'd soon see that first, most people don't really have an understanding of what conservation is, and second, that is maybe because conservation is often so complex and is built up from so many different layers of involvement that it is no wonder it could do with a bit of a PR makeover. The truth is that it is a highly important area of science, backed up and supported by lots of robust (and complicated) research. Conservationists are not 'animal cuddlers', they're biologists, botanists, veterinarians, mathematicians, economists, geologists, physicists, chemists and a host of other people from science, banking, business, education and other fields of expertise. To make something such as conservation work, you don't just need people who know about plants and animals.

Conservation has changed over the years. It has gone from something that almost resembled a battle and worked on a basis of 'us against them', with conservationists being on one (the 'good') side and local people being on the other ('bad') side. It's easy to think that, for example, to help sharks being targeted and killed in Madagascar by

---

1 Don't ask a conservationist, that's cheating. They know the answer… it's hard, tiring and too often ends in failure.

2 Although this is definitely not a self-help book, if you do ever find yourself applying for conservation work (especially if you're paying to go) and it's advertised as involving lots of contact (and cuddling) with baby animals, then it might be a good idea to look elsewhere and spend your money on a different project. Let's just say no more about these types of opportunities and animal exploitation. Agreed?

local people, surely we should go after these local 'bad guys', arrest them, lock them up, smash their fishing gear and tell everyone else what happens if they catch internationally protected species. But what if I said that this particular local community had specialised in hunting sharks for generations and that they had only ever caught the number of sharks they needed to feed their community until a few Chinese[3] businessmen came in, gave them new (better) fishing gear, and more money than they'd ever seen before in return for killing hundreds and hundreds of sharks, just for their fins? The fins are cut off,[4] dried and sent abroad to be made into an expensive but tasteless soup so rich businessmen can impress their rich mates. Are the poor fishermen in the Madagascan village still the bad guys here, or are they now the victims? Are they being exploited the same way as the sharks they're hunting? What would *you* do if your monthly wage went up from a little over a few pennies to several hundred pounds, dollars or euros? You could buy your family more food so that your children don't go to bed hungry. Maybe you could finally pay for that medicine your granny desperately needs to help her get better, or maybe you could replace that awful leaky grass roof with a proper one that keeps you warm at night. What would you do? Would you still care more about the sharks? As you can see, it immediately gets more complicated the moment you start considering the local people and their lives. There

---

3 This is difficult. I'm not picking on certain countries or people here, but the truth is that some countries and cultures do target particular species. Lots of countries (including ours) cause environmental damage; China happens to cause lots of problems for sharks. And elephants, rhinos and pangolins. And lions, sun bears and a fair few others.

4 The fins are cut off while the shark is still alive. So many are caught that they are not wanted for their meat. Instead, they are thrown overboard and sink to the seabed. Sharks are tough, so they don't die straight away. It is said that they can take up to two weeks to slowly die, sometimes from starvation. Some estimates state that, every year, over 100,000,000 sharks are killed for their fins.

will always be people who say that the animals being saved are more important than the local community involved. Those people are idiots and the truth is they don't make good conservationists. But in fairness, conservation *used* to be like that. It was more of a battle and in most cases, less science was involved. Too often we saved species or habitats at the cost of local people, often with terrible consequences. When I was growing up, there were a few very famous conservationists who were tragically killed doing what they loved most. George and Joy Adamson dedicated their lives to saving leopards and lions in Kenya and both were murdered in separate attacks. Dian Fossey lived in Rwanda and was the first person to successfully work with wild mountain gorillas (although the legendary zoologist George Schaller gave it a good go before her, but with less success). Dian habituated, studied and saved these incredibly beautiful and gentle African apes and, like the Adamsons, was killed by a so-called fellow human. Here is not the place to get into what was right or wrong in their work[5] but the truth is that Dian, George, Joy and so many like them lived, worked and sometimes died in a time when conservation was more centred around opposition than collaboration, where local communities were often seen as something to overcome rather than help. Without the help of these early conservation pioneers, we wouldn't be where we are today, but I am glad that conservation, and the way we look at it, has changed.

So, it is (hopefully) obvious that conservation isn't about cuddling cute little animals[6] and that it has moved on from a time when we

---

5 Because it's not fair that they can't answer. Each of them got things wrong and each got things right. It is easy for us to look back and say what *should* have been done, but the truth is that they were all great conservationists in so many ways.

6 If that's what you're looking for, then go to one of these cat cafés that keep popping up everywhere. This is in no way me supporting cat cafés… I think they're weird. The bad weird, not the good weird.

focused on only the animals. I've already said that conservation is based on authoritative scientific support and have hinted that it involves collaborating with local communities but, in truth, it is highly complicated, highly stressful and nearly always highly specific to that particular project. It makes sense that a shark conservation project and one focusing on saving chimps would be different[7] but two chimpanzee conservation projects can be very different from one another if they are in different parts of the same country. The types of habitats, the local (human) communities, climates, cultural beliefs, religious beliefs, level of education and even the quality of the roads can and do all make a difference in how you plan a project and its chances of success. Lesson here is to make sure you have nice roads.

As well as having worked in Africa and Asia in great ape conservation, I do a lot of teaching nowadays and not just because I like to talk and know I have an audience that cannot leave for the next two hours. I teach at university and I love it. Teaching allows us to explore ideas, discuss problems and debate how we can overcome them. My favourite module to date focuses on the role people play in primate conservation and (rather imaginatively, if I do say so myself) is called Anthropology and Conservation. It has nothing to do with how to dart a baboon[8] or how to count the number of gibbons in a forest by listening to how and when they sing. It's all about the people.

This is the sort of stuff we cover, which in turn means this is the sort of stuff we need to do in order to help save primates in the wild. Do a little thought experiment for me and think of three different species threatened with extinction and worthy of some serious conservation

---

7 For a start, there is usually less need to snorkel in a forest looking for chimps.

8 If you ever find yourself needing to learn just how (and how not) to do this, then please, please, please read *A Primate's Memoir* by Prof. Robert M. Sapolsky. You may not learn all the finer details needed for darting, but you'll have a great laugh reading about how it can go so horribly wrong.

loving. Okay, done that? Now, I've not had professional training as a mind reader but I'm guessing your list doesn't include anything like a slug, frog or vulture. I'm 100 per cent assuming plants weren't even an inkling in your head (and yes, I did say 'species' and not 'species of animals'). I'd be willing to bet that your list included animals such as tigers, polar bears and of course our old favourite, the panda. Am I right?[9] There appear to be favourites among those species most 'worthy' of conservation support and usually, the average person will think of animals before plants. I'm guessing your list of animals didn't include the humble European eel, the bizarre kakapo from New Zealand or the tragic vaquita from Mexico. These are critically endangered[10] and represent a fish, bird and mammal that arguably need more help than the beautiful tiger, the stunning polar bear and the cute panda. So why do some species get more help when others are in as much, if not more, need? It seems unfair. Well, it makes more sense when you think of conservation as being like a business. The simple truth is that we do not have the money or energy needed to support every single species that needs our help. When you start seeing celebrity-led newspaper campaigns to protect slugs or TV ads asking for money to save lampreys then it will be a good (but strange) day for conservation. Think about it: if you want to save some special and rare species of snail in a local forest, do you think you're going to get a lot of support? I'll tell you now, the answer is that regrettably, you will have a hard time raising that money. And, if you do raise enough, it will be unlikely that you will be able to save anything other than the snails and maybe the plants

---

9 If I guessed all three, then I do expect some sort of prize!

10 In terms of being worse off, 'extinct' is the next category in the chart used to grade conservation status in nature. We call it the UICN Red List and it's not a list you especially want to score high on.

they feed on, unless you are very, very lucky.[11] Now, imagine there are also badgers in the same forest. Cute and cuddly – their stripy faces are simply adorable. They're an instant win[12] and it's easy to imagine how much more easily the money will roll in. Even if the badgers don't need as much help, focusing on them may be a better tactic. Not only would you probably be more successful in raising money but, by using the badgers, you would also indirectly be able to save lots of other animals, plants and other organisms within the forest. It's all about the flagship species and the umbrella species.

A flagship species gets its name direct from history. Way back in the olden days, before we could show the world via Instagram what our breakfast looked like or tell strangers how we're feeling in a tweet, we had to be inventive in terms of how we communicated. If one country decided to scrap with another country and both had navies, then knowing who was in front of you was a real worry. The answer was that both sides would have used a flagship, which was exactly what it sounds like – a ship with a great big flag attached to it. The flagship sailed at the front of the fleet and let everyone know who the ships belonged to, avoiding that awkward situation where either you start firing cannons at your mates or invite a bunch of pirates over for brunch. A flagship species acts in much the same way. It is chosen because it can be used to represent lots of other species.

---

11 Partula snails are a great example of an exception here. They're a real conservation success story, not only because, through captive breeding in zoos, their numbers are back up and, for now, they've edged away from the threat of immediate extinction but because there wasn't a fluffy mammal in sight – Partula snail breeding and reintroduction programmes show that you don't need a spinal cord for conservation to be successful.

12 Unless you are of the persuasion that badgers should be culled. If you are, you're probably not the greatest fan of this conservation book (or rigorous science) but thanks for sticking with it this far.

It's often a political decision[13] and flagship species are chosen for their popularity. They represent something bigger and helping them can help others. The best example of a conservation flagship species is the WWF panda. Think about it, the World Wildlife Fund (WWF) works all around the world, covering countless projects, with countless species. Yet it is represented by the panda. It's not as though the WWF works exclusively with pandas. Similarly, in the UK, we have regional wildlife trusts. There are currently forty-six of them.[14] Their overall logo is a badger[15] and yet again, these trusts work with insects, flowers, amphibians, reptiles, fungi, birds, trees and amphibians, not *just* the cute and cuddly mammals. And there it is, in part, at least.

Similarly, there are the umbrella species. This is a similar idea, where one species benefits others; but whereas the flagship species is intentionally selected, an umbrella species can pop along almost accidentally. Flagships can be used to help other species in terms of financial support, but protecting an umbrella species has a more immediate impact on other species. A flagship can be used to help unrelated and unconnected species anywhere in the world. An umbrella species is different, because it helps those other species living within the same habitat or ecosystem. It serves just like its namesake but rather than protecting you from the rain, it saves other species from numerous conservation threats. If you look at my conservation history, it's not difficult to see that I like the big and iconic stuff – sharks, orangutans and of course those chimpanzees. There isn't a snail or nudibranch or

---

13 And it really *is* a decision – flagship species don't happen by chance. They're the rock stars of the conservation world and, as with any good superstar, there's a whole horde of people behind the scenes, making them the success they are.

14 Loosely, each one represents a different county but sometimes some trusts join up and sometimes new ones form.

15 Although it might seem like it from my two examples, a flagship species doesn't have to be black and white to pass the test and qualify.

sparrow in sight. Part of that is because I have always believed in the use of both flagship and umbrella species. When I lived in Uganda, my project was within the largest and oldest mahogany forest in the whole of East Africa. In that amazing ecosystem, we had something like 290 species of butterflies and around 360 different bird species, not to mention the hundreds of reptiles and amphibians, plants and fungi. It was (and still is) one of the most important places for biodiversity in that part of the continent. Imagine trying to get enough money and resources to save every plant, fungus, animal in need of help. It would never have happened. The distressing thing is that many of these species are in desperate need of help and some are found nowhere else on the planet or, if they are, then in just a few locations maybe.[16] But chimpanzees can act as protective umbrellas and saving them leads to better protection for other species within that habitat, as well as the habitat itself. One big difference is that an umbrella species doesn't always have to be big and majestic or cute and fluffy or even that 'popular'. Condors, ladybird spiders, swallowtail butterflies, green turtles and mountain chickens[17] have all been successfully used as umbrella species.[18]

There are plenty of other conservation tools that are used in various ways and many of them focus on the successful involvement of people. Every time I teach conservation to a new bunch of students, I always ask how many of them want to work in conservation. As you might expect,

---

16 One of my favourite examples, found nowhere else in Uganda, in only a couple of places in East Africa and just a handful of locations throughout the rest of Africa, was a very small, brown (some might say nondescript) bird called Puvel's illadopsis (*Illadopsis puveli*). It never ceased to amaze me how far some visitors came just to see this little bird. I grew to love it.

17 You are just going to have to research this one for yourself. I'll give you a clue – it's most definitely not a chicken.

18 Although, for the record, they're all awesome (and cute) in my book.

rather a lot of hands go up at this point. I then follow with a rapid 'Who wants to work with people?' and always chuckle as most of those same hands shoot somewhere beneath the desks, without a trace. When I tell them that in conservation, working with people is not only the biggest and often most difficult hurdle, I remind them that it is also frequently the most important aspect of the work of a conservationist. Remember, if we ignore the people, then our chances of success drop rapidly. So, how do we go about this? First of all, much of what we do is at what we call a 'grass-roots' level. Like the real thing, grass-roots conservation means you work way down the line, where a lot of the activity is going on and where a lot of the problems might actually start. It's often here where the greatest differences can be made. Of course, it's important to work with national governments and international regulations when working with chimp conservation, for example, but you must absolutely work at a grass-roots level too. Why? Because first, none of us like being told what to do, do we? Whether it's teachers at school, the boss at work or our elected governments, it always feels better if we believe we have some say in the matter. Including people at a local level hands over that power and responsibility to the communities. A subtle but important transition is made. You change things from a situation where people are *forced* to save the chimpanzees raiding their fruit trees, even though it might be much easier to kill them, to one where the same people are *empowered* and become conservation stewards, looking after the chimpanzees instead. Second, at a grass-roots level, you can make all the conservation work specific to that area or (human) community. Grass-roots conservation includes local communities (and their needs and fears) at the centre of a programme, alongside the species being focused on.

Creating a sense of empowerment and stewardship is great but if the chimps in the neighbouring forest are still eating your fruit and yet again, you are facing the prospect of a poor harvest, then they're still not going to be your favourite neighbours. As conservationists, we have to find

A future again. Lei Lei and the others have a bright future ahead, now they are safe with the Desmonds.

ways to cultivate (and often incentivise) a positive attitude towards species at the centre of conservation management. One of the most direct ways in which we can do this is through alternative livelihoods. If we want people to stop illegally cutting down forests or hunting primates or selling illegal bushmeat in markets, then it has to be a successful relationship and, like any successful relationship, both sides need to benefit. It's simply not enough to tell them that it is morally[19] or legally[20] wrong. Regardless of what you think about loggers or hunters or illegal market traders, these jobs bring in money for these people and their families. If you want them to stop, then you are going to need to find

---

19 Because the painful truth is that it is not necessarily wrong. Some cultures kill and eat apes and have always done so. Some kill tigers because they attack their livestock or, worse, children. Successful conservation often means the need to look at an issue with different eyes and not only see it from our own cultural perspectives.

20 Very often, the local, national and international laws aren't known, not just by local communities but I've met police and judiciary who have not known it is illegal to own a chimpanzee, for example, in their own country. The solution here is to offer training opportunities for all levels of local law enforcement.

them new work. The actual workings behind alternative livelihoods are, at worst, a logistically complex nightmare and at best, a wonderful mish-mash puzzle (mainly because that sounds less daunting). It's one of those situations where you may have to take into consideration all manner of cultural, socio-economic and logistical factors. Rather than explain in fine detail how the methods behind alternative livelihoods work, I'll tell you about one of the nicest examples I've come across.

A problem in lots of areas in the tropics where there is a concentrated conservation focus is the issue of hunting with snares. These long strands of metal wire or cable are tied to a sapling, which is bent over and staked into the ground. The end of the snare is formed into a loop. The animal stands inside the loop. Trap is sprung. Sapling snaps back. Leg is caught tight. Hunter returns. Animal is killed. Hunter's family is fed. It's not an especially ethical or painless method of hunting but it does work and has been used as a technique for innumerable generations the world over. Setting aside the idea that snares are not a good thing, there are three additional considerations. First, they are indiscriminate. They can catch anything from an elephant shrew[21] to an elephant. The problem in our forest was that hunters were after forest buck, duiker and other antelope, bush pigs and the occasional buffalo, if they were feeling especially brave. While great apes are intentionally targeted in many places across Africa, they were not hunted in Uganda. But this didn't stop them from stepping into these deadly wire loops and one of my least favourite statistics is that back in the early 2000s, around 50 per cent of wild chimpanzees in some forests had significant trauma from snares, meaning they had lost a hand or foot,[22] or worse.

---

21 Yes, they are a real thing. Check them out. They're bizarre little quirks of evolution and there was nothing funnier than hearing one come wondering through the forest, loudly foraging through dry leaves, only to freak out and run off once they realise you're sitting silently nearby.

22 I remember hearing about one old male in a different part of the country who had

The second consideration is that modern snares are made from metal. Everything from electrical wire to bicycle cables is used. This significantly worsens the impact of this already effective hunting method. Chimpanzees are very strong and when caught, are often able to pull the snare from the ground and walk off, with it still attached. Then the snare gets to work. It tightens more and more and over the next few days or weeks, infection, and often gangrene, sets in. If the hand or foot doesn't drop off, then the infection may kill the unfortunate victim. So, what to do with modern snares? Lots of things have been tried. Paying ex-hunters to collect snares works where you don't pay them for every snare collected, because this quickly leads to more snares being laid in the forest, so more money can be collected. Anti-snare patrol teams are effective and are widely used but cause anger and can lead to reprisals from local communities. Some solutions work in principle but were never allowed to develop. The pioneering Professor Vernon Reynolds from the University of Oxford suggested replacing metal cable with previously preferred liana vines, making them sturdy enough to catch most mammals but weak enough for chimps to break. This was a win-win idea. But after suggesting that a project could even help grow the vines and teach local hunters how to use the older techniques again, the project was shot down by local authorities as it was seen as supporting illegal hunting activities.[23]

The third consideration with the wire snares is that there were so, so many of them. They were everywhere and, in some cases, we're talking tonnes rather than kilos. I haven't forgotten the lovely example for alternative livelihoods – I am getting to that. I'm just setting the stage

---

lost a hand and both feet to snares. He would still follow the other chimps and would even try to climb up trees at night to build his sleeping nest. This story broke my heart and although I never met this old male, I think of him often, still.

23 For what it's worth, I think this was a great idea.

here. I think we're all in agreement that snares are bad now, right? We were looking for a holistic way to tackle the snare problem and it was proving tricky. I was away from camp for a few days, 'down country' visiting the charity HQ. We had a horde of visitors and volunteers and as usual, I set about getting to know the new faces. One was an Australian artist called Eric. We instantly got on, through a mutual appreciation of sarcasm and certain cold beverages, and before long were lamenting the problem of snares. I had recently been involved in a few de-snaring trips where we had successfully removed snares from wild chimpanzees,[24] and it had got to me. I was angry, frustrated and annoyed and couldn't see a way to resolve the problem that would benefit everyone. Looking back, the solution was so simple, but when Eric suggested it, it was as if the clouds had parted and a giant cartoon finger pointed straight at the answer. 'Why don't you use the snares as material for making crafts? Make bookmarks or greeting cards or something.' Wow, simple as that. It sounded simple, but how do you turn a rusty, tetanus-covered piece of death wire into something you'd like to buy for your granny to show her how nice Africa is?

Next morning, I found out. Overnight, Eric had taken a piece of wire from a snare, cleaned it, cut it down to size and shaped it into a simple but effective outline of a walking chimpanzee. It was fairly small, but it looked great. The next bit was a buzz but before long my brilliant boss, Debby Cox from the Jane Goodall Institute, had a whole plan formulated. We were going to make greetings cards and export them to posh hotels in Uganda but also to international zoos. The card was going to be made by local communities (from recycled paper, corn

---

24 I'm lucky enough to have been involved with one of the first teams to successfully do this in East Africa. It was stressful but an amazing feeling to be able to help in these desperately dismal situations.

husks and old banana leaves[25]) and the chimp outlines would be made from snare wire – a poignant reminder of the tragic threat they faced. This idea was a guaranteed win from the start. All we had to do was train people from local communities – turn hunters into craftsmen, sell the cards worldwide and make enough money to stop a whole load of people from hunting with snares. We'd already lined up a few buyers[26] and we headed out to an area where snaring was a problem.

Gave them the spiel: 'We all love chimps, don't we?'

Choruses of 'Yes' all round, in response.

'We should save them from extinction, right?'

Shouts of 'Oh yeah, for sure… right on!' echoed around the village.

'So, we should stop this awful snaring business, shouldn't we?'

'Erm, yeah… of course.' Awkward sidelong glances. Feet were shuffled.

'Anyone here ever go out hunting with snares?'

'Definitely not. Never. Hate 'em.' Lots of vigorous head-shaking.

'So, anyone got any snare wire?'

'No way!' We were (very) vocally assured that there never was or never would be anything resembling wire that could be used for snares in the area. Nothing even looking like wire.

'Aww, shame,' we said. 'We have some card, some tools and some designs. We were going to give you a dollar fifty for every card you guys make and we were going to buy as many as you could produce. We just need some wire.'

It was genuinely as though we were magnetic. Metal wiring and cable appeared from every direction. People ran off and came back with

---

25 If you've never made paper, then give it a go. It's messy but fun, and you end up with a very cool piece of paper. Yes, sometimes the simple things are the best in life. Go make some paper, then you'll see.

26 It's very important to do this if you're ever in this situation – otherwise you're left with hundreds (or even thousands) of unwanted cards, baskets or dreamcatchers.

armfuls of the stuff, grannies opened long coats to expose reels of different thickness wire hidden in secret pockets, kids dashed to dredge kilos of bike cable from the village well. 'Stuff like this?' We smiled and got to work. We trained a group of local gents[27] how to make the paper, how to create different chimp shapes and how to sew them on to the cards. It was a fun few hours, first of all reassuring the men that yes, they could do craftwork and still be manly[28] and then, yes, it does need to actually look like a chimp in order for us to sell these things – that random blob you handed me looks more like an amoeba than a chimpanzee. When we were satisfied with the first dozen or so chimp snare outlines, we left, all cheers, smiles and handshakes, and said we'd be back in a few weeks.

An essential point to remember here is that we needed to see a drastic decrease in the number of snares being set in the forest. The idea was that, with more money, they could afford more meat and eventually money that could be spent on home repairs, medicines, education and maybe some of life's little luxuries. Hopefully, they'd earn more from crafts than they ever would from hunting bushmeat. But the bushmeat hunting did need to stop.[29] We informed them that we were working with several neighbouring communities along the forest edge. We'd be making random trips to the forest and if we found evidence of snaring, then we'd not be buying cards for a while. A savvy, newly qualified

---

27 It wasn't that we were intentionally being sexist, it was just that the men were the problem. They were the ones doing all the hunting.

28 Wow, that male ego, hey! Some of my team nearly fainted when I first cooked for the rest of the staff. It was curious how, over the next few months, almost all the other guys decided that it was in fact okay for men to cook. We had to promise not to tell their wives… it's not as if they wanted to cook at home, or anything.

29 It only works like this in areas where bushmeat is a luxury item. In areas where it is classed as *subsistence* hunting, where they really need the meat to survive, then communities generally need a bit more of a helping hand in various ways.

craftsman asked what if sneaky neighbouring communities planted snares in their area. We hadn't really thought about this, if I'm honest, but never one not to have an answer, I said they'd have to regulate and police one another. It made a lot of sense when we thought about it – we couldn't afford teams to police the forest and anyway, it would have been a monumental task. By watching each other, they effectively did the job for us. When we could look in the forests, we very happily found that snares were few and far between.

When we returned to that initial village for the first time, we were pleasantly surprised[30] by the resourcefulness of humanity. Those five or six blokes we had originally trained were all apparently creative entrepreneurs, just waiting to unleash their artistic flair and business capabilities. Stacks and stacks of cards had been made. It appeared that there couldn't have been a single piece of unused metal wire or unwanted corn husk within a 20km radius. Despite (quite unfairly, I must say) thinking that this quantity of cards could only have been made with some poor and shoddy workmanship, we saw instead that the bloody things were all perfect. What's more, they'd created new designs 'so that people can buy more than one'. And these were perfectly made too. Now worrying that this small band of men had not slept, eaten or moved in several weeks in order to make so many cards, we asked how exactly they had managed the impossible. It was simple. All they'd done, they said, was to train a bunch of other people, thereby turning a sleepy little African village into a thriving hub of craft-based industry. Great.[31]

What's more, they realised that sewing wire chimps on to card was fiddly work, best suited to little fingers. So, the kids helped after school.

---

30 Please read 'thoroughly overwhelmed' here.

31 If you can't tell by now, this is not my genuine 'great'. This is definitely my sarcastic 'great'.

Killer crafts. Turning deadly snares into beautiful greetings cards helped not only wild chimpanzees but also local human communities.

Washing and drying out old paper, corn husks and banana leaf to make the pulp needed for the cards was a bit too much like housework for some of the men. Wives and grannies, they found, were much better at it. Suddenly, there was a whole production line present, based on skilled labour. The men had decided that crafts using metal wire were okay after all. Especially if these crafts made a ton of money. As a result, we gave more specific requirements, learned to be more exact in future projects, and set about contacting more zoos to buy more cards.

This effective case study shows nicely how alternative livelihoods can work and how they can be tailored to overcome a specific problem. It also shows what can happen when an idea is embraced. I'm happy to say that, for a few years at least, the snare cards were a big success. There are plenty of examples whereby local communities are empowered through conservation programmes based on alternative livelihoods. In Tanzania, the Jane Goodall Institute has had huge success with 'chimp-friendly' tea and

WWF has done the same with 'gorilla-friendly' coffee.[32] Conservationists from Bristol Zoo have been involved in lemur-friendly chocolate in Madagascar and in Kenya, Save the Elephants helps produce elephant-friendly honey.[33] All these examples benefit local species or habitats but, importantly, also the local communities. In an ingenious example, in several regions across western Africa which have had lots of problems with bushmeat, communities were encouraged to farm and eat cane rats. They were already eaten locally, so farmers were taught ethical welfare practices, and after raising them they were sold at local markets. Not every example works in every situation, which is why it is so important to know your local area, get to know the people and understand and respect their culture. When conservation is being threatened by business, then see conservation as a business. You want local stakeholders to invest; they want to make money; economic incentives are great at getting people involved and cooperating. And like the very best businesses, if your conservation work with alternative livelihoods is unique, interesting and benefits all involved, then you're more likely to be successful.

Another way to work with local people is through what we call community development programmes. It may not be through alternative livelihoods in particular, but here, you still work closely with the community. This is a broad area of conservation and we could easily discuss it for hours. Loosely, it can be broken down into two main areas: 1) helping local communities get what they physically want, such as building wells or clinics or buying farmland, and 2) helping them get things that are less material but arguably more

---

32 These are examples of 'buffer crops'. Rather than grow tasty things such as fruit and sugar cane close against the forest edge (which you know will be eaten by chimps and gorillas, for example), planting things such as coffee, tea, chocolate and soya beans acts as a buffer zone. These buffer crops are not eaten by wild animals, and can be sold commercially.

33 These animal-friendly products are different to coffee picked by monkeys or pooped out by civets. Those are definitely not animal-friendly products.

important. The most important would be education. I'm probably going to rant on here, which is something I'm remarkably good at, but for me, in any conservation project, the thing upon which everything else is built is education. If you don't do this properly, then I can almost guarantee that either your project will fail or you'll be stuck with a programme that you can never leave as it slowly but surely emotionally drains you and the budget, neither of which is a good outcome. But if you can work *with* the community and help implement a good and successful education programme, you will have a unique opportunity to help those people, and the species and habitats you are ultimately trying to save, in ways you couldn't imagine. So much has been written about conservation and education but I'm not going to go there or pretend I can teach you anything, other than to say it's essential and wherever possible should form part of the foundation of your work in conservation. You can work with women's groups, village elders, teachers, the police or the community in a large, mixed group. You can obviously also work with young people. By working with schools, colleges and universities, you're helping to create and strengthen a vast network of people who will grow up to look at the world around them in a completely different (and hopefully better) light.

In one of my projects, education featured heavily, and it was during this time that I was introduced to the concept of pre-, post- and post-post-evaluations. The idea is simple. You do some sort of activity, such as lessons. In order to see how effective it is, you assess either the knowledge or attitudes of the participants before and after the activity to evaluate whether any changes are visible, which would show that the activity has been successful. The 'post-post' bit goes further and can be done weeks or months later, to see whether any changes in knowledge or attitudes, as a result of the activity, have been retained. If they have, then you are on to something. We wanted to look at the attitudes of local kids and how they viewed the forest. I can still see them turning up in a bus we'd hired.

Devotion. Caregivers such as Jenneh provide invaluable care for the orphans and are showered with love in return.

All in unfathomably white shirts with clean backpacks which looked too heavy for such little legs. I remember what it was like to go on a school field trip when I was seven or eight and it was always great fun. We used to look forward to a day away from school for months ahead. Judging by the faces I saw that day, I can only assume they'd been told they were off to meet the Child Catcher from *Chitty Chitty Bang Bang*.[34] They did not look happy. I then did the awkward thing where I dialled up my excitement and happiness levels a good forty-five notches. Again, this did not help. It dawned on me that it was the forest itself that was scaring the kids and that their pre-evaluations were startling. The record sheet we gave each of them had multiple sections, with 'tick the words that describe how you feel' and 'list the benefits of the forest' being just two. My favourite was a row of five faces, going from the deepest level of unhappiness and desperation on the far left, 'teenage indifference' in the

---

34 If you're too young to remember this, google it… if not, then you'll know just what they looked like.

centre and a smiley face on the far right that I had only ever experienced when my folks brought home a puppy one day.[35] The pre-evaluation forms were an eye-opener for me. Almost without exception, every child had listed words associated with negative connotations. The forest was scary, dark, horrible, terrible, dark, dangerous. Really dark. The benefits were purely economic, with bushmeat and timber being the only advantages these kids saw to having one of the most important forest habitats in the whole of East Africa on their doorstep. As for the faces… there weren't any 'puppy-happy' faces circled. It was safe to say that these kids did not want to be here. Maybe my empathy levels are low or possibly I'm a bit of a monster, but either way, I marched those sixty or so terrified kids straight into their worst nightmare, with a 'puppy-happy' smile plastered across my face.

And they loved it. Of course they did. We cut a vine and let them drink the water from it. Crouched to look at the military lines of safari ant soldiers and showed them which tree bark was historically used to make clothes for their kings. We saw and heard all manner of fascinating birds, managed to annoy some monkeys and even found a beautiful chameleon. This time, almost every sheet listed 'happy' words – now the forest was fun, friendly, green, nice, important… it was a textbook-worthy change in perception. Now, rather than an economic resource, the kids were saying that this ecosystem benefits from giving oxygen, generating local weather and 'being at home to biodiversity'[36] to having cultural importance and health benefits for local people. As for the face-o-meters, they were all (with one or two diehard exceptions) big, happy, maximum smiley faces. How good is that? This showed that

---

35 If you're wondering, I still have that same happy face, which is usually reserved for dogs. It's fair to say I have a dog-related problem.

36 This is a direct quote and made me so happy. It's as if they'd read my mind. Either that or they wanted to leave that forest so much, they would've said anything.

even with a brief forest-based activity, a simple community project can have significant impact. We then went all out and did the post-post-evaluations about six months later and I'm pleased to report the forest was still a good place, animals represented something more than lunch and there were great big smiley faces all round. With this sort of community engagement, you are playing the long game. Rather cynically, there is a train of thought that goes along the lines of 'work with kids, the adults are too set in their ways and are already a lost cause'. But kids grow up and can become teachers, scientists and politicians and will have both a better understanding of conservation and greater appreciation of its benefits. Singling them out in this way is tactical and in terms of impact, does work, but I would never say that it is not worth working with adults in education programmes for conservation work as, for me, the key is to make education work as broad and inclusive as possible. All this talk about focusing on the younger generation in order to achieve conservation goals may seem like a sneaky approach, covertly changing cultural ideas and ideals one generation at a time, and maybe it is, but when we're talking about the current conservation crisis with our great apes, then I think we're okay to use whatever (ethical) methods we can to make sure these kids grow up with chimpanzees in their world.

My take-home message is this – lots is being done and lots can be done to help ensure that chimpanzees inhabit our tropical forests for millennia to come, and at the centre of that work is a fundamental and close working relationship with local communities. Through alternative livelihoods, community engagement and education, we can help save our closest cousins. All across the range, there are dedicated people working with satellite imagery, law enforcement, schools, genetics and other conservation tools to prevent the threat of extinction. We still need more people to join us and I'm happy to see more and more young conservationists joining the ranks all the time.

# FRIENDS REUNITED?

## Heading back to the beginning

How many more? Although Bui is now safe, how much longer will we need to rescue chimps from markets and confiscate them from homes?

Chimpanzees are iconic. Enigmatic in a way few other species are. Capable of tender moments of quiet reflection and breathtaking acts of aggression, they are a fascinating, enthralling and sometimes uncomfortable mirror held up to our own species. Our shared ancestry, genetic features and behavioural repertoire gives them, as our closest living relatives, a unique position within the animal kingdom. But it might not be enough and our quadrupedal forest cousins may be set on a path to extinction, immortalised by film and documentaries, with invaluable specimens housed in museum stores and only a few zoo collections acting as the last bastions of day nests and pant-hoots.

Imagine a world without chimpanzees for a few moments. It's a sorrowful prospect, isn't it? How will we explain to our grandchildren what happened if we allow chimps to slip into the annals of history? How would we justify it to ourselves? With so many species facing the threat of extinction, it would not bode well if we were unable (or unwilling) to save one with so much charisma and so many links to ourselves. The threats continue to increase for chimpanzees at an alarming rate and although their use in biomedical research, for example, has been greatly reduced in recent years, their involvement in the illegal pet trade continues to take its toll, with an estimated average annual value of the market for live traded African apes of around US$9 million. Additionally, the trade of live orphans instead of body parts such as horns, ivory and skins, which is a much more common form of wildlife trafficking, seems especially harrowing, adding extra trauma to the babies' suffering. The international commercial bushmeat trade continues to grow while governments and border agencies are seemingly unable to tackle it. With one estimate predicting that around eight thousand gorillas, bonobos and chimpanzees are killed every year for food, the desire for the perceived delicacy of ape meat in cities around the world is seriously contributing to already dwindling populations of African great ape species. Yeah, things are tough, but there *are* glimmers of hope, small but piercing patches of success among the pervasive apathy and gloom that surrounds us. Work is being done around the world by governments, universities, companies, community groups, schools and, importantly, by individuals, showing that there is something each of us can do, regardless of how small we are or how quiet we think our voice is. Through my work with the Jane Goodall Institute, I have had the honour of meeting and hearing about so many young conservationists from every part of the world. A young man who found meaning in nature and uses it to give strength to others inspires me. A young woman who speaks quietly and eloquently, stirring crowds of thousands to march for a better world, gives me hope. And another young woman, who sat outside her parliament day after day, defying her parents and her school until finally the government and then the world took notice, makes me believe we can still make a difference. If these three young people can make such a ripple around the world, just imagine the flood we would cause if we all worked together. I'm always moved by a story I heard from Jane a few years ago. A Roots & Shoots[1] group had been set up in the Democratic Republic of the Congo. It was the first group in the country and the thing they really wanted to achieve was to reforest a sacred hill. The forest had been cut down, leaving this locally important site stark and ecologically vandalised. The young group leader needed to gain permission from the resident militia in Goma, a volatile area that has seen the most awful ravages of war and the worst that humanity is capable of. Although permission was granted, the militia leaders insisted on sending soldiers with the kids. With saplings donated by the forestry

---

1 These groups are set up by young people all around the world. Playgroups, schoolchildren and university students all form Roots & Shoots groups, each one unique, sharing only the need to base their work on projects helping species and habitats. They are an amazing example of what young people can achieve.

department, the fifteen children set off to the hill, shovels slung over their shoulders, accompanied by four AK-47-wielding soldiers. The tree-bare, sun-baked earth was so hard the children were unable to dig. One of the younger ones began to cry. After twenty minutes, one of the soldiers placed his gun on the ground and started digging. After half an hour, all four had set down their weapons and were replanting trees with the children. This ability to set our differences aside and willingness to work together to make the world a better place is what will, I believe, enable us to save coral reefs from bleaching, protect the polar ice sheets from melting and ensure ancient forests are not all felled. It will mean we can prevent some of our most iconic sharks from being continuously overfished, that wolves are no longer persecuted and that we carry on with great ape cousins by our sides rather than relegating them to the oblivion of extinction.

Wishful thinking? Maybe, but we have to remain positive and optimistic, as without that, what's the point? If we lose hope, then everything we're fighting to save is already lost. There are dedicated charities working around the world, armies of volunteers making a difference and scientists making it their lives' work to help. Our governments need to get their act together and commit to change, not endless and meaningless sound bites to want change in ten years' time, but now. With global climate change and the threat to our natural world being the most important issue of our time, we need to see people who are willing to save us leading our countries and our governments. We don't have time for shallow, self-serving, divisive politicians filling our lives with hateful walls, spreading hurtful distrust to our closest neighbours and creating fear of those different to ourselves. As they fill our newspapers with an ever-increasing political pantomime, more and more ice caps, forests, reefs, lagoons, meadows, woodlands, savannahs, jungles, mangroves, plains, downs, tundras, prairies, estuaries, streams, lakes and rivers are all being destroyed. As much as we need better leadership, though, there's so much each of us can do as individuals. Every single person has the ability to help and each of us can make the world of difference to our planet. Shop locally and buy seasonal, local foods where you can. Recycle wherever possible, reduce the amount of waste you throw away, and definitely cut the amount of single-use plastic you buy and use, as much as possible. Little things such as using a canvas bag for shopping, a reusable cup for coffee and not taking plastic drinking straws really do help. Plant some wildflowers, leave a patch of your garden to grow wild and use your bike or walk more. Every little action really does help, and the world will thank you for it.

And chimpanzees? What does their future look like? I don't know. None of us do. What I am certain of is that they are under greater threat now than ever before. I know that the next few years will be pivotal and that their future is in our hands. I also know that never before in the whole history of their existence have they had so many people fighting their corner. People like Jane Goodall, Jimmy and Jenny Desmond and so many others, dedicating their lives to saving chimpanzees. I look at the Desmonds and they fill me with hope. These conservation heroes, who have given up so much, leaving their home, their friends and their families to save apes half a world away. I admire them, love them and am continually inspired by them, genuinely believing that if the western chimpanzee is to survive in the wild, it will be down to the Desmonds and people like them.

While writing this book, I returned to Uganda, making the trip back to the place I consider my second home for the first time in over ten years. I went for various reasons but one was that I wanted to see Pasa again. I felt nervous and full of worry at the idea of seeing her after so long. Would she have forgotten me? Would the passage of ten years leave me simply as another anonymous face staring at her? Or would she remember that silly boy who had let her groom the back of his

Looking back on it all. Even the dog is called Mini Monkey.

hand through the bars all those years ago? Over a decade had passed and we are both different people now, admittedly from different species but still people nonetheless in my eyes. Uganda remains as beautiful as the day I left it. I made a pilgrimage across the country, seeing chimps wherever I could. I finally heard pant-hoots at the foot of the thickly forested hills in Bwindi, home to the legendary mountain gorillas. I saw an isolated group eking out a life in the Kyambura Gorge (known locally as the 'valley of the apes') and watched as tourists got too close to the most habituated chimps I know, in the renowned Kibale Forest, where fancy cameras, expensive walking boots and untold viruses are carried to within sneezing distance of these relaxed apes. I visited my old home in Budongo. I spent a few days at my old site, which had changed a fair bit since I was last there. The staff had all gone and the camp at Kaniyo Pabidi is far poorer for that, so I went to see if I could find them. Justin had died from an accident and poor Joshua was taken by HIV. Old Sippi is now a farmer but John and Chombe had moved to just outside the national park. I tracked down Sauda, as I couldn't bear the thought of seeing *my* chimps with any guide other than the ones I'd worked with and lived with before. I spent three days looking but finally found her. We embraced and caught up for hours. She filled me in on all the news, good and bad, and it was as if I'd never been away. She was always the best guide at my site and jumped at the chance to get back into the forest. Next day, we entered the forest and it was perfect. The humidity wasn't too bad and tendrils of early morning mist unfolded like spectral ferns. The floor was soft with a thick carpet of leaves, bright pink *Thonningia* buds poking through, beautiful but painfully sharp. Huge trees towered around us, like giant pillars in an impossibly large cathedral dedicated to nature. I identified an emerald cuckoo by its call, surprisingly myself and making Sauda laugh. The rasping, raucous call of cicadas pierced the stillness every so often, with the halt of their noisy crescendos only accentuating the silence that followed. I heard the chimps calling. My chimps. Chimps that I, along with Sauda, Sippi, Joshua and the others, had habituated and followed for so long. We found them in the canopy of a mighty fig tree – a *Ficus mucoso*, if you're wondering. We sat on the ground (well, I lay flat on the forest floor[2]) looking up, binoculars trained into the leaves, where an old black hand curled around a small bunch of pale yellow fruits. Three or four chimps sat on a branch, gorging themselves, with another four or five close by within the same canopy. It was a tall tree and they were maybe 40m up, but I looked over to Sauda and did my 'quizzical eyebrow' thing. 'Is that really…?' She chuckled and said yes, it was Maria. Already old when I worked there, Maria was unmistakable and now ancient. Surrounded by younger adults and a couple of kids, her back and arms were entirely grey. She moved slowly and her face was deeply etched with lines but it was her, named after Sippi's mum back in 2006. Maria was still alive, still having kids, it seemed, and still thriving. It felt good to know our project had succeeded in securing the chimps in this part of the world, thankfully. I left my old forest happy and reassured that, for now at least, wild chimpanzees are okay in places. I headed down country, towards the airport, where I was due to fly to West Africa for another visit to the Desmonds. I had one last detour to make.

I made the boat trip across Lake Victoria and was back on the island sanctuary. I was with Lilly Ajarova, the sanctuary director and one of the most dedicated conservationists I have ever met. It was a surreal day back on the island, but then again, nothing ever was normal there. I had already seen most of the chimps during their lunch feed. I tossed some fruit to impatient outstretched hands as they came down from the forest and although I counted plenty of

---

2 I always used to love lying down in the forest, flat on my back, looking up and only occasionally regretting that I hadn't checked for safari ants.

The beautiful early morning light in Budongo Forest. This forest is home to lots of different species and was where I and my team habituated wild chimpanzees.

Me with Sauda, who is quite possibly the best forest guide in the world. Leopard print never used to be part of the project uniform… she didn't seem to think it would be a problem in the forest. Where real leopards live.

*Thonningia* buds in Budongo forest. These weird, spiky little plants are commonly found there and were often sat on. They are used right across Africa, in everything from soup flavouring to poison, which seems risky for at least one of these options.
Photo: Cat Hobaiter

Pasa enjoying a bowl of porridge.

familiar faces, I couldn't find the one I was searching for in particular. Almost dreading the answer, I asked where Pasa was. My heart lurched when Lilly said there had been a problem, but I laughed when I heard what that problem was.

Of course I'm biased, but I do think Pasa is one of the most intelligent apes I know. This was only reinforced by what I heard next. She always liked being where people were and used to regularly escape when she was young. Growing old, it seemed, had done nothing to dampen her spirit. Lilly told me they were fixing an oversight on their part in the design of the electric fence, which my favourite non-human friend had discovered. Pasa had started bringing long, flat branches from the forest to the fence. She would dig a hole under the fence, using the spade-like branch, and when the hole was big enough, would place the flat branch, which now served as a shield, on her back, so that the electrified wire wouldn't touch her. She'd shimmy under the fence and would be free to go and see her mates, the humans. I don't think I've ever been prouder. After doing this on two or three occasions, she was spending time in the large sleeping quarters, while the fence was made Pasa-proof.

I walked over to where she sat close to the bars and called out her name. She was much bigger now. Maturity and a good diet had turned this odd, scrawny kid into a big, strong adult. Her face had lost its childhood paleness and was coal-black, with more wrinkles than I remember. Although to be fair, I am probably greyer and more wrinkled that she remembered too. She looked up and showed me the most vibrant, richly coloured brown eyes I've seen. They lingered for a second, maybe two, before glancing away. I was more wary of Pasa now. She was a big animal, capable of injuring me. I definitely wasn't going to fall for that hand grooming thing this time. I didn't even know if she remembered me. Then she looked my way again with her shiny chestnut-brown eyes, and she extended her arm. She looked at me and I at her. Large black leathery fingers gently stretched out towards me, invitingly…

For more info on Jimmy and Jenny Desmond and the amazing work of Liberia Chimpanzee Rescue & Protection, check out their website:

www.liberiachimpanzeerescue.org

If you're interested in the work of the Jane Goodall Institute or want to get involved with a Roots & Shoots group, here's how:

www.janegoodall.org.uk

And if you love all things primatey and either want to one day study them or are working with them now, then there's no better place to start than with the Primate Society of Great Britain:

www.psgb.org

Proceeds from this book will help chimps in Africa.